The Turkey Shack

A JOURNEY TO LOVE

Dave Snyder

Avenson Publishing
Lead, South Dakota

Cover photos:

Front: Dave at 12 years old, with his new dog Pep, in front of the Turkey Shack.

Back: The entrance gate to Pathways Spiritual Sanctuary.

David Wayne Snyder/Avenson Publishing
21793 Juso Ranch Road
Lead, South Dakota 57754
www.PathwaysSpiritualSanctuary.org

Book Layout ©2017 BookDesignTemplates.com

Ordering Information:
For details, contact: www.PathwaysSpiritualSanctuary.org

The Turkey Shack/David Wayne Snyder—1st edition 2018
ISBN 978-0-692-12230-3

Contents

Dedicated

to my wife
Jan Avenson Snyder

without whose help, support and encouragement
this book would never have come to fruition

Author's Preface

I'm a guy who wears Carhartt jeans, with pliers in the pocket. I also was the CEO of a $65 million agribusiness and the Executive Director of a $100 million-plus science research laboratory during its startup. Along the way I had spiritual experiences that mystified me. I didn't shave my head, don robes or join an ashram. My life continued, but it was changed.

In 2010, I created Pathways Spiritual Sanctuary on my ranch in the Black Hills of South Dakota. Based on my history, you might think I'm an unlikely person to create a spiritual sanctuary, so let me tell you up front what I am not. I am not a guru. I am not a psychologist, philosopher, theologian or a person with a degree in any field that would seem relevant to spirituality. I do have bachelor's and master's degrees, but in agricultural economics. I remain the guy in Carhartts, a Nebraska farm kid, who happened to have some extraordinary experiences that allowed me to see a new world of love, compassion, tolerance and forgiveness.

This book is the story of that journey—a story that begins in a tin shed called the Turkey Shack.

Dave Snyder
Founder
Pathways Spiritual Sanctuary

PART I—THE JOURNEY BEGINS

CHAPTER 1

Dave's Story – The Turkey Shack 1954

It's a hot, humid summer night in Nebraska. I make my way through the thick juniper bushes growing next to our farm house. It's pitch dark. I creep along hugging the side of the house to avoid being discovered. I peek into the corner of the large picture window, so I can see into the well-lit living room. I peer in, careful not to be seen. My dad, Wayne, my stepmother, Percy, and my sister, Karen, who is two years older than me, are playing with my little half-brother, Tim. I watch them laughing at Tim's antics. He is almost 2 years old. I have lived here for a few months and I long to be in the house with them. I begin to cry.

I leave the window, but instead of walking the half a mile through the cornfield to the tin shed where I sleep, I walk to the machine shed. It's my refuge. My place of comfort. It smells of grease and fuel, tractors and tools. I sit on the dirt floor in the dark building with my back against the rear tire of our Ford 8N tractor. I place my head in my hands with my elbows supported by my knees, which are pulled up to my chest. Tears fall on my cheeks. My sobbing grows in intensity until my entire body shakes.

I cry until I can't catch my breath. "I want them dead." I repeat, louder and louder. "I want 'em dead, I want 'em dead!" My dad.

My stepmother—she is NOT my mother! I want them all dead! I am not plotting murder. I don't intend to kill anyone. It's just the only way I can imagine getting back to my other family on the farm where I have lived for the past seven years. That's where I belong—with that family on that farm, where I was happy. But I've been taken from that home. Now I'm living with my dad and his new wife, and their baby boy and my sister.

After a few minutes I calm down. My crying subsides. I wipe the tears off my cheeks with my T-shirt sleeve. I stand up, brush the dirt from my jeans and climb onto the seat of the tractor. I shift to the left side of the seat stretching to search for the clutch. I find it and manage to push the pedal far enough to shift the gears in the dark. I imagine driving the tractor through the fields. As I turn the steering wheel from side to side and shift gears, I feel like a grown man tilling soil, planting corn and mowing hay. I feel better. My fantasy ends, as it always does, and I realize I must go to the tin shed. I get off the tractor and walk out into the darkness.

I can't see anything except what's in front of me. From memory, I find the small path that winds through the pine and cottonwood trees surrounding the farmstead. I walk past the giant cottonwood tree that marks the entrance to the path through the cornfield. I shudder and my heart beats faster, as it does every night when I head into the cornfield. The path is ten feet wide, just wide enough for a tractor. It's August, so the corn bordering the path is over six feet tall. It seems like twenty feet tall in the darkness.

My heart pounds. I'm scared. I have a small flashlight in my pocket, but I don't turn it on for fear the light will allow someone to see me. I pull my baseball cap down on my forehead, hoping that makes me less visible. I pretend the towering corn stalks are not there. A slight breeze rustles the stalks. I quake with fear. Someone could be after me.

I walk at a fast pace with my head bowed and my eyes fixed on the path ahead. I start counting my steps to the tin shed. That calms me, but I can't concentrate long enough to count all the way. My fear returns. When I see the tin shed, I run as fast as I can, open the door and dash inside, closing and latching it behind me. I look under the bed, then climb onto the old mattress fully clothed. I pull the worn blankets over me and put my head under the pillow, pulling it over my ears. My beating heart slows down. The fear ebbs. Then comes the waves of loneliness. I fall asleep.

My new family calls that 6-feet by 8-feet tin shed the Turkey Shack. It is my bedroom from spring through late November. It is for the turkey guard. Me! Our 10,000 turkeys are raised outside in a large, fenced pen dotted with portable shelters. At night, coyotes or other predators threaten the flock. In the fall, as Thanksgiving approaches, the predators might include humans.

In the Turkey Shack are all the necessities the "guard of the turkeys" might need: a short metal spring cot with a thin mattress and a couple of blankets, a double-barreled 12-gauge shotgun with shotgun shells, an oil lantern and a large flashlight. If predators awaken the turkeys, their commotion will awaken me. I would then get up and confront the threat with my shotgun.

But I'm not a guard! I've fired the shotgun once, and it bruised my shoulder. I'm a little boy hiding my head under the pillow trying not to hear scary sounds—night after lonely night.

I am nine years old.

CHAPTER 2

Wayne's Story – Harvest 1946

One August night in 2016, my dad came to me in a vivid dream. He died in 2012, at 95, but in the dream he was alive and standing in front of me. He wanted me to experience his emotional turmoil in the summer and fall of 1946. He said for me to experience what he had felt during that most difficult year I needed to go back to that time and become him.

Suddenly, shockingly, the dream's perspective shifted. It's 1946 and I am my dad, Wayne, a young man standing in a Nebraska cornfield on an October afternoon, handpicking corn.

I walk along the rows, mindlessly picking an ear off each stalk and tossing it into my old wooden wagon pulled by two draft horses. I grab the shank of each ear with the hook of the husking glove on my left hand. Twisting the ear with my right hand, I toss it over my right shoulder into the wagon. Walking to the next cornstalk, I repeat the process—cornstalk after cornstalk, row after row. The repetition is meditative. The horses stand still until I reach the front of the wagon. Then they move forward one wagon length. I don't give them a command to move. Somehow, they just know.

The previous days had been warm and sunny, Indian summer days, with a gentle breeze blowing through the corn stalks. Today is different. The clouds are gray and the wind has shifted, now coming from the northwest. The temperature keeps dropping as I pick the corn along a row that disappears over the hill to the west. Every time I turn to toss another ear into the wagon, the wind bites my face. I worry that a late fall storm is coming or, worse yet, an early winter blizzard. I move with determination. I must get this corn into the crib to pay the hospital bills that are stacked on my desk at home.

Cold air reminds me it is the middle of October, and the number of good harvest days remaining could be few. Then it hits me. Today is October 11. My stomach clenches. I stop picking and lean my forearms on the wagon's sideboard. I hold my head in my hands, fighting back tears. The warm days had lifted me out of my depression, but now it returns with a vengeance.

Today is the two-month anniversary of the day my wife, Geneva, last looked into my eyes and said "I love you" as she lay in a hospital bed. Within minutes she was gone.

Memories return and with them the weight of all the pain I've been carrying for the past two months. Sometimes it retreats, but it always returns, often in moments I least expect. Grief crushes me, immobilizes me. I lean against the wagon for support, facing into the cold wind. My knees tremble and I cry like a child.

Geneva was 25 when she died. Twenty-five! That number played incessantly in my mind in the months before her death, ever since doctors at Mayo Clinic told us there was no cure for Lupus, the rare disease that had ravaged her petite body. For months I watched as my beautiful wife, who always had so much vitality, withered away. How could this happen? She was the most loving person I knew. During the agonizing months leading to her death, she never once complained. Her concern was always for me and our two children. We both cried when she told me how, as she held each child for the last time, she tried to explain she had to leave them. She wondered if they understood. Part of her hoped they did not. Our daughter Karen was not yet 4 and son Dave was 22 months old when she died.

I kick the wagon wheel in anger. How could a loving God allow this to happen? Neither of us had done anything to deserve this painful ending. Our children did not deserve losing their mother. Our prayers had not been answered. Once again, I doubt there is a God. And with no God, there is no heaven. My beautiful Geneva was gone forever. We would not be reunited. She was just gone.

But I also remember that in the moments before she died, she turned toward me. For what felt like an eternity, she silently looked deep into my eyes. She seemed oblivious to her pain. Then she smiled as she told me the children would be cared for, that I would be fine and that I must remarry. She told me she loved me and turned her head away, her eyes fixed on the ceiling above her.

Listening to her final words, I was overcome with emotion. As I reached out to hold her one last time, I saw her look up and back over the headboard of the bed and mutter the words, "Let's go." I looked up. I saw nothing, but in that moment, it was clear to me that someone was there to take her. My grief eased. I had a flicker of hope there was a God. I felt consoled, even reassured, that she was not gone forever, but, that she had moved on to another place. I sat there holding her inert body. I was engulfed with her presence, as though she was holding me, suspended in a deep feeling of love. I have thought of those last moments every day since her death.

Standing in the cornfield, leaning against the wagon, I feel Geneva holding me. As my crying subsides, my emotions come in waves, shifting from anguish to anger to love in a cycle that has tormented me these past two months. Will it ever end? There cannot be a loving God.

Since her death, I have no desire for companionship, even when family and friends check to see how I am doing. I have no interest in talking. Instead, I find a fragile peace in being alone on my small farm.

I walk across the land carrying my pain like a sack of feed on my back. Sometimes I follow the path to the hillside in the pasture, where I sit down and cry. The cattle are my comforters. They gather round me as I sit on the ground and look up at the sky searching for answers. At first, I assumed they thought I had feed for them, but now I realize they sense my despair, especially when they lay down beside me.

A gust of wind catches the brim of my cap, and I look up at the threatening sky. A second wave of grief overwhelms me. Tomorrow is October 12, little Dave's second birthday. I must call my sister Marian to let her know I will not be able to drive the 110 miles to Pilger for his birthday. I need to assure her I will come visit as soon as the corn is harvested.

My thoughts return to Geneva's funeral. My sister Marian had seen Dave running on the gravel driveway. He fell and cut his knee. He got up crying as he looked for his mother. At that moment, Marian decided she must help me. She knew I could not care for the two children and fulfill my farming responsibilities. She offered to keep Dave until the harvest was finished, or longer, so I had time to heal.

I look at the ears of corn in the wagon. They are an affirmation that she was right, I could not work this farm alone and care for two little children.

Life was a blur the first weeks after Geneva's death. I don't remember my other sister Edith coming to get daughter Karen. I don't recall a goodbye, but I do remember the anguish I felt when I looked into her empty bedroom that first night after she was gone.

The October afternoon has slipped away, and I decide to quit for the day. As I climb into the wagon for the ride home, my mind drifts back to the day I took Dave to the farm near Pilger. It was less than three weeks after the funeral. My father offered to take us, and he helped me put the crib in the back of his pickup. Dave sat on the seat between us holding his teddy bear. He always had a lot of energy and seldom could sit still for long. Even at this young age he seemed to have more of his mother's personality than mine, especially his mother's liveliness and quick laugh. He was already talking in sentences, but on this day, he was quiet. His inquisitive looks made me wonder what he knew.

As we headed north towards Pilger, I saw little Dave watch my father shift gears in the pickup. His eyes went to the clutch as my father depressed it, and then to the gearshift as it moved and then back to the clutch as it was released. His attention was fixated on each shift. I believe he understood the entire process.

My father seldom spoke during that drive. Even though Snyder men are typically not talkative, I felt his silence was out of respect for me and my distress. When we turned off Highway 275 near Pilger, I wondered for a moment if he felt my pain. When I glanced his way, I noticed the tight grip of his hands on the top of the steering wheel. I knew he could see my gaze, but his eyes stayed locked on the road ahead of him. A large tear rolled down his cheek. I placed my arm around my son and lifted him onto my lap to hold him one last time. Tears ran down my cheeks as we drove up to my sister's house.

Our goodbyes were gut wrenching. I wanted to change my mind but knew I couldn't. I remember Dave's questioning gaze as I closed the door of the pickup and we drove down the drive. I turned and saw him standing on the lawn watching us leave without him. Did he understand? Would he ever forgive me?

My thoughts return to the present as I guide the horses into the barn. I notice a broken steel wheel in the barn that I had welded back together. I try to imagine my broken heart welded whole once again. Today my heart is still broken, and it seems there is no one, not even a God, who can fix it. I am alone.

I am 28 years old.

CHAPTER 3

The Alpine Ranch
1993

arly one Thursday morning, in late February 1993, I headed
to the Black Hills of South Dakota in search of property. I
was living in Pierre, South Dakota, three hours away. I had
a Black Hills National Forest map with me, on which I had circled
the general area I wanted to scout, looking for the ranch of my
dreams.

I had been thinking about retiring in the Black Hills since the
1980s. Why the strong attraction? Perhaps it's nostalgia. After my
mother died, I lived with my aunt Marian and uncle George Rennick for the next seven years. Right before I moved back to live
with my dad, Marian and George took me and my three cousins to
the Black Hills for a summer vacation. That trip marked the end of
the happiest time in my childhood. Later, when I moved my own
family to Pierre, the Black Hills became a favorite vacation spot.

But I think my attraction to the Black Hills was more than nostalgia. I always felt at home there. At peace. I never tired of the
drive to this beautiful range of mountains. I loved walking in the
forest, with few intrusions of man-made sights and sounds. I found
these walks in the Hills intimate and embracing. I was alert to the

natural sounds of the forest and I often experienced a profound sense of calm.

My dream was to retire to a small ranch of maybe 160 acres. Over time, my image of this property became clear. It would be located at the end of a maintained road but surrounded by the Black Hills National Forest, so there would be no visible structures on neighboring property. The ranch would be one-half forest and one-half meadow, with a spring-fed stream that flowed all year. There would be a small pond on the stream. There would be electricity to the property and a well for drinking water. It would be in the northern Black Hills so there would be snow in winter, and it would be within 10 or 15 miles of a town.

I knew the general area to look for my dream ranch, in a small area of the Northern Hills. Most of the map was colored green, which meant it was part of the Black Hills National Forest. Private land was colored white so it was easy to pick out. I was discouraged by how little private land there was in this particular area. No parcels met my criteria. One property looked promising, but I discovered a small acreage was carved out of it, and there was a home on it. A second parcel met my criteria, except a highway ran along its western border.

After several hours of studying the map and driving back roads, I noticed a tract that was surrounded by the Black Hills National Forest. Even better, it was at the end of a road. Why hadn't I noticed it earlier? It felt right. As I turned off the highway and began driving the mile and a half to the property, I had a strange but powerful feeling that this was the ranch. My ranch. I could feel it in my gut. My heartrate increased in anticipation.

Over two feet of snow covered the ground. The road had been cleared, but it wasn't good, making me thankful I was driving my four-wheel-drive Jeep. The road in my dreams was well-maintained and I began to have doubts, but as I neared the property, my belief that this was it returned. I reached the gate, and my heart sank. I saw dilapidated buildings, junk and trash. There were cats, rabbits, geese, goats and barking dogs. I looked closer and saw more junk protruding from the snow. But there were also other buildings, and a barn. This was, indeed, a ranch.

I looked beyond the farmstead and across the beautiful expanse of undisturbed snow blanketing what had to be one of the most beautiful mountain meadows in the Black Hills. My eyes followed the slope of the meadow to the eastern edge, which was framed by a pine and spruce forest. Aspen groves bordered the south and west edges of the meadow. This must be the ranch.

The gate was open and smoke was coming from the chimney of the old ranch house, so I drove in and knocked on the door. A woman appeared and peeked at me through the small window on the door. She opened it a crack. I tried to make small talk. She was not friendly, but I gathered from our conversation that she was a tenant. She would not give me the name of the owner. As I gazed across the snow-covered meadow, I decided to drive into the nearby town of Deadwood and visit the Register of Deeds office to find out who owned the property.

Finding the owner was not difficult and I was encouraged to discover that he lived in nearby Rapid City. A phone book revealed his number and I picked up the receiver to call him. I started to dial the number but clunked the receiver back on the hook. I was scared. It reminded me of when I was a teenager calling a girl for a date. What if I was rejected! This was the only property I saw on the map that met all my criteria. What were the odds that this man would be willing to sell? What if his wife didn't want to sell? What if the price was too high? What if he wasn't home? I was paralyzed, but reason soon returned. I picked up the receiver again and dialed his number. A man answered.

I had not thought how to approach the subject, so I stammered a bit trying to figure out what to say. I took a deep breath and asked if he would be willing to sell the ranch. There was a moment of silence on the other end of the phone. "This is a coincidence," the man replied. "I was just putting pictures together because I planned to list the property for sale tomorrow." Could this be true? I asked the price. It was reasonable. As a businessman I figured I'd negotiate later, so I said nothing. Besides, I hadn't inspected the entire property. I asked if he would allow me to cross-country ski the ranch that afternoon. He agreed. After a quick lunch, I rented skis and headed back to the ranch.

I spent the next three hours skiing the entire 200-acre property. I was amazed at my energy. I skied to the highest point on the east side of the property feeling no exertion. When I reached that high point, I turned to the west and gazed at a long view, over the meadow to the mountains beyond. I knew at that moment: this was the ranch and I would own it. It was an exhilarating feeling.

I called the owner that evening. I told him I was interested and, remembering to negotiate, we agreed on a price. The mechanism of the sale was complicated. It involved a land trade and a resale agreement with my business partner, Dave Luers, so I called him. The next morning Dave and our wives drove out from Pierre to inspect the property. We all agreed it was right. On Saturday morning we met the owner for breakfast at the Holiday Inn in Rapid City. He was unmarried, the sole owner, and he owed no money on the property. He preferred a contract for deed and we agreed to an interest rate and other terms of the contract. He was a building contractor, so he had a contract form on his computer. After breakfast, Dave and our wives returned to Pierre while I went to the owner's house to execute the contract for deed. I gave him a check for the down payment. Before noon on Saturday, just two days after first laying eyes on the property, we had purchased a 202-acre ranch in the northern Black Hills.

The ranch was larger than I had envisioned, but it was at the end of a road, and it had a running stream that flowed all year. The stream originated from a spring that emptied into a small pond.

The ranch was surrounded by the Black Hills National Forest. Other than the buildings on the ranch, no man-made structures were visible. The nearest private property was a half mile away. Rural power came to the residence, and a well supplied domestic water.

The one element that did not match my vision was the road into the property. It required four-wheel-drive access for much of the year. To my surprise, after acquiring the property, the county highway engineer informed me the road was scheduled for upgrade and improvement. The roadbed would be raised and graveled and there would be new culverts. The work was done the following summer.

As planned, I bought my partner Dave's half interest in 200 acres, and he kept two acres for a second home. So, in addition to being next door neighbors in Pierre, we became neighbors on the ranch as well.

I had now acquired the ranch that would become the home of Pathways Spiritual Sanctuary. I also began to recognize the power of intentions, thoughts and prayers. In the ensuing years, I continued to experience focused intention evolving into physical reality.

And how the events of my life are inter-connected.

CHAPTER 4

Pathways Spiritual Sanctuary
2010

I opened Pathways Spiritual Sanctuary on July 17, 2010. As I developed the concept, I discussed it with several friends and acquaintances. Most of their reactions were polite but reserved. "It sounds nice," they said. They were sure "some people would appreciate it." I could hear their skepticism. Others were not so reserved. "Are you nuts?" one male friend asked. "I thought you were a businessman."

Maybe he had a point. My plan was to set aside 80 acres that would be open to the public—friends and strangers alike—free of charge. I would build the sanctuary myself. From personal funds I would pay the costs of construction, maintenance and operation. And that's what I did. Since 2010, Pathways Spiritual Sanctuary opens each year in May and closes the end of October. Even though I don't advertise it, thousands of people have visited the sanctuary. Most people hear about it by word of mouth. Why do they come?

Maybe it's the land itself. Pathways is at the end of a road, on the south end of my ranch. The Black Hills National Forest surrounds three sides of the sanctuary, and the remaining acreage of the ranch borders the rest, so it's isolated from development. At an elevation of 6,100 feet, the terrain is a mixture of mountain meadow and forest, with stands of aspen, ponderosa pine and Black Hills spruce. Except for the sounds of nature, it's a silent place. These natural features are common in the Black Hills, but somehow this land seems different. From the first day I set foot on this ranch in 1993, I've felt a powerful positive energy here—the energy that seemed to propel me across the ranch when I skied it on that first visit.

Pathways offers a unique way to experience that positive energy. At the entrance, I built a large, solid wooden fence with a gate that is a portal to what lies beyond. Once inside, visitors may walk the mile and a half path that meanders through meadows and woods. Benches along the path are tucked away in quiet places and provide guests the opportunity to pause and reflect or simply experience the natural space. An outdoor labyrinth, modeled after the famous labyrinth in the Chartres Cathedral in France, built around 1100 is in a clearing in the aspen grove. In other places along the path, bronze and wood statues evoke a connection to spirit. Plaques offer quotes from contemporary and historical figures whose words have influenced me and many others. These features help create an environment that invites visitors to spend time walking, sitting, contemplating or healing.

Since the first day Pathways opened—strangers and long-time friends alike—have asked the same questions: why would I open my private land to the public and why would I do this free of charge? I fumbled for answers, saying something like "it needs to be shared" or "it's just something I choose to do." But the more I thought about it, the more I realized my answers fell short of the complete truth.

In September 2013, a close friend suggested I record the story of creating the sanctuary for a project called StoryCorps, whose mission is "to preserve and share humanity's stories to build connections between people and create a more just and compassionate world." StoryCorps recordings are done in an interview format, and their mobile studio was coming to nearby Rapid City. I reserved a one-hour recording session. My friend and interviewer, former journalist Bill Harlan, was at the time communications director at the South Dakota Science and Technology Authority. Bill had worked for me when I was executive director of the science authority. He also knew about my business background in large-scale farming. We sat down in the recording studio on October 2, 2013.

Bill's first question: "So, Dave, you often describe yourself as a pig farmer…How (did) a pig farmer come to create a spiritual sanctuary? I see no connection. Please connect the dots." I stumbled through my answer in much the same way I had when trying to explain Pathways to visitors and friends.

After the interview, I returned to the ranch and walked the path. Why did I create Pathways? Maybe I was the one who needed to know the answer. I had spent more than two hundred thousand dollars on the project and months of labor, without knowing if anyone would use it. Pathways is not a tourist attraction, and it never will be. It's just open and free. Perhaps I WAS nuts!

I've spent the years since the interview trying to answer that question, and the search led me to reflect about my life. I discovered that the further down the rabbit hole I went, the further I had to go. I opened Pathways 17 years after I bought the ranch, 56 years after my first summer in the Turkey Shack, and 64 years after my mother died. Parts of my journey to Pathways have been painful, but I've also experienced a vivid and dramatic spiritual world that, in the first 50 years of my life, I did not know existed. The real and complete answer to the question "why Pathways?" lies in the interconnectedness of many events in my life. I realized to answer the question for others, I would have to unearth and expose much about me that few people know.

Was I willing to tell all?

CHAPTER 5

The Pilger Years
1946–1953

When Bill Harlan asked me to connect the dots between corporate hog production and creating a spiritual sanctuary, I pondered a long time. I came to realize the dots went all the way back to 1946 and the death of my mother. I was not quite 2 when my dad left me with my aunt Marian and uncle George Rennick. Their farm was 110 miles north of Dad's, near Pilger, Nebraska.

I once told a therapist that I wasn't conscious of feeling abandoned at that early age. I was just a toddler, and I blended in well with the Rennick family. George and Marian were great parents. Marian, a school teacher, was one of the kindest, most patient and caring person I have ever known. George loved to tell jokes and had a deep belly laugh. I now had a new brother and two new sisters. Teresa was one year older and I viewed her as my protector. Will was a month younger and the most curious about my arrival, maybe because we were so different. He was quiet, I was talkative. He may have learned to speak up more because he had to say no to me so often. Will and I became best friends and every day we played for hours. Becky was three years older, and I looked up to her as the wise one.

I was too young to work on the farm near Pilger, but I experienced farm life there. In summer, the four of us roamed around the farmstead and in the fields. We played in the grain when it was harvested, and Will and I farmed in our large sandbox. We got along by dividing the sandbox into two fields, one for each of us. Will was the careful one, and his toys forever looked new. Mine looked like they had farmed a thousand acres. I also had ideas about improving my toy implements. Sometimes those improvements involved a hacksaw and resulted in a destroyed implement that never made it to the improved stage in my imagination.

I've loved tractors and machinery for as long as I can remember. I often watched George go back and forth across a field, either tilling the soil, or planting, or cultivating corn. I dreamed of driving that tractor. Calendars from implement dealers with pictures of the new tractors, intrigued me. I flipped through the calendar months studying every detail of each machine. When Will and I went with George to the implement dealers for parts, I'd go outside, climb on a new tractor and drive it back and forth across the fields of my imagination.

We had adventures, too. One day Teresa, Will and I rode off into a corn field on hobby horses we made from sticks. We got lost, and Marian couldn't find us. Frantic, she called the sheriff for help. By the time we found our way home we were bedraggled and tired. Out of the cornfield we came, at a slow but ordered gallop. We laughed about it when we were older because, despite our exhaustion, we still felt the need to ride our stick-horses instead of just dragging them. To our relief we were greeted with hugs, not anger. On another occasion, Will and I decided to help George by washing his car before he had to drive to an important meeting. It had rained the night before and we used rags soaked in water from puddles in the yard. The more we worked the dirtier the rags. When George saw his mud-caked car, we could tell he was shocked. He knew we could tell, too, but he didn't scold us. Instead, he sat us down, one on each knee, and thanked us. Then he wiped off the car windows and drove to his meeting.

On Saturday mornings, Aunt Marian baked bread. She had four small bread pans and it became a tradition to bake a separate loaf for each of us. We were called into the house when the bread came out of the oven, and we'd run in laughing and giggling. We each ate our entire loaf, then ran off to play again. The smell of that hot bread and the taste of it with melted butter is with me to this day.

I remember my seven years in Pilger as the happiest time of my childhood—life with the Rennicks was warm and loving. And yet, sometimes I felt like an outsider. When I was introduced to people, someone often explained that my mother died and my dad couldn't take care of me. At Christmas, sometimes one gift came from my dad, not from George and Marian. They were gifts from someone I barely knew. Because 110 miles separated Dad's farm from the Rennick place, and because Dad had no one to help him with the livestock chores, his visits were infrequent. We saw each other on some holidays or at family gatherings.

But there was a story playing under the surface of the carefree life I enjoyed in Pilger. Somehow, I didn't quite belong. I felt separate.

And the feeling of separation would get worse.

Will, Dave, Teresa and Becky

Dave, Will, Teresa and Becky

CHAPTER 6

Back to the Future
1953

M y carefree childhood in Pilger, Nebraska—which lasted
seven years—ended in late summer 1953, when I moved
to a farm near Lincoln to live with my dad and his new
wife.

Dad had married Olive "Percy" Percival in October 1951. Photos taken during their courtship suggested Dad had healed from the
loss of my mother five years earlier. Dad had always planned to
take Karen and me back to live with him, but he and Percy decided
to leave us with our interim families while they adjusted to their
married life. Percy, who was in her early 30s, had never been married. My step-brother, Tim, was born the following October, so our
return was delayed again, while the newlyweds adjusted to having a
new baby.

Meanwhile, in Pilger, I did not want to move. Cousin Will and I
were inseparable, almost like twins. Cousins Becky and Teresa were
like sisters. We were involved with school and church activities and
playing with the neighbor kids. I hardly knew my dad, and my sister
Karen felt like a distant cousin. Dad and Percy and our surrogate
parents also struggled with the decision, but they worried about
what Karen and I would think later, if Dad didn't take us back. In

the summer of 1953, the decision was made for us to move back to live with our dad. Karen and I moved in early August, so we could adjust to our new lives before school started. By then, Dad and Percy had been married almost two years. In October, Tim would be 1 year old and I would be 9. Karen would turn 11 in November.

Adjusting to our new combined family was difficult for everyone. Karen and I were strangers to Dad's new family, and they were strangers to us. Percy was learning how to be a parent to her own young son. She and Dad didn't know how to parent us, the older kids. Dad was farming, which meant working long days outside, away from all of us. My new school was difficult, too. I entered the third grade in the little town of Walton, a few miles east of Lincoln. My classmates had known each other since kindergarten. I was the new kid. My behavior at home didn't help, either. I was making life difficult for everyone, maybe to make them give up and send me back to Pilger. I teased and tormented Karen. I also made it clear I didn't want Percy to be my mother. I unfavorably compared everything she did to what Marian did, and I let her know about it.

Baby Tim got most of the attention. Percy was thrilled to be a new mother, and Dad would lay on the floor of the living room playing with Tim—something he never did with me. Except one Sunday afternoon, when I got a new baseball and glove, Dad played catch with me. That memory stands out because it's the only one of its kind. Dad was always gentle and kind, but also quiet and uncommunicative. He didn't know how to interact with me, maybe in part because of his broken heart. Later in his life he told me I reminded him of my mother, which brought back the pain of his loss.

More than anything, Tim's birthdays stood out. They were glorious celebrations. Percy decorated the house, and her entire family attended. Tim wore a new birthday outfit and received gifts from everyone. Home movies were made. When I watched those movies years later, I was embarrassed at my antics. It was obvious I was trying to get attention. When my sister Rebecca (Reb) was born two years later, her birthday parties were also festive celebrations. In contrast, Karen and I didn't have parties. No friends, no grandparents, no other extended family. Percy did bake us birthday cakes. We received one major gift, such as a shirt or dress, and maybe a couple of small gifts. Other than a rendition of Happy Birthday, there wasn't much of a celebration. One of the saddest memories of my childhood was captured in a photo of Karen sitting on the floor with her birthday cake. She is dressed in an attractive skirt and sweater, but she is alone. There are no presents. No decorations.

When I discussed this with Dad and Percy later in life, they told me they hadn't thought that birthdays would be important to older children. They apologized, and said they wished we had spoken up. I also learned how difficult this transition had been for Percy. She and Dad had discussed many times whether bringing us back was the right decision. They even considered letting us return to our surrogate families. As a kid, I was unaware of their concerns.

I was focused only on what I wanted.

Percy, Karen, Tim, Dave, and Wayne Snyder holding Reb

CHAPTER 7

Becoming a Farmer
1954

I made new friends at school, but I no longer had Will to play with. When I got off the school bus, I was alone and unhappy. My loneliness, however, began to dissipate in an unexpected way. Dad took me with him as he did his farm chores. At first, I trudged along kicking stones, but as I was given my own chores I began to realize this was more real than farming in the sandbox with Will.

At that time, Dad was farming with my Grandpa Snyder. In addition to raising crops, they raised 10,000 turkeys each year, and in the 1950s that required hard manual labor. Dad and Grandpa were both methodical workers. They never seemed to be in a hurry. They focused on each task, talking only about the job at hand. I began to enjoy working with them. And while guarding turkeys at night had been traumatic for me, by the next summer, at 10, I was accustomed to my nights in the Turkey Shack—even though I was often still scared and lonely.

As I was assigned more chores, I began to focus less on playing. One day in late summer my transition from play to work took an exhilarating turn—I got to drive a tractor. My long-held dream! We had a Ford model 8N. Even for its day the 8N was small, with less than 20 horsepower. Decades later, the largest tractor my business used had 525 horsepower and weighed 25 tons, but this little Ford could not have seemed larger to me on that day. Dad showed me how to put the tractor in gear and told me how to release the clutch. He didn't know I had done this many times, alone at night, sitting on the same tractor in the dark shop. On this first day of driving a tractor, I was pulling a drag harrow, so it would be difficult to damage anything. Dad started me off in the small field that separated our house from my grandparents' home which was about a quarter mile away. I let out the clutch with a jerk, looked back at Dad, and headed toward Grandma Snyder's house. I had watched men drive tractors since I was a toddler. Now I felt like a man.

Grandma was outside hanging clothes on the line. I called to her, and she looked at me with a mixture of surprise and concern. I was all smiles as I waved to her. Near the end of the field, I turned to drive back to Dad. We had not practiced this part, and my turn was too sharp. I looked back just in time to see the harrow riding up the tractor's rear tire. I panicked but pushed the clutch and stopped the tractor. Had I not stopped, the harrow would have continued up the tire and landed on top of me. My pretend farming in the shop must have saved me. Dad ran across the field to me. I was still shaking as he explained how to make a wider turn so the harrow wouldn't climb the rear wheel. Then he sent me off to the other end of the field. With each wide turn I gained confidence and it wasn't long before I had harrowed the entire field. I didn't want to stop, and since Dad was now doing another chore, I kept harrowing.

That summer I also got to drive the 1-ton Chevy feed truck. Dad let me drive it back to the feed shed after we delivered feed to the turkeys. To start the truck, you depressed a starter button which was located on the floor to the right of the throttle pedal. Because I was small, to reach the starter I had to pull myself down by grabbing the lower part of the steering wheel. This was not easy.

I pushed the starter with my toe while using my heel to depress the throttle. The truck had a floor-mounted manual shift lever which was a long reach for my short arms. As I drove, Dad sat beside me, laughing at me peering through the steering wheel while trying to keep the truck on the road between the rows of corn. Maybe that was his way of playing.

Karen worked inside, helping Percy with Tim, but we did share one major task. Dad had a thousand chickens. Each day Karen and I collected eggs from underneath the laying hens, while the hens pecked mercilessly at our hands. In the evening Karen and I took the collected eggs and, one by one, cleaned them with sand paper. Then we weighed them and put them in separate crates marked small, or large or extra-large. There were a lot of eggs—it seemed like thousands every week.

Dad and Grandpa also raised sheep. We had only cattle and pigs on the farm at Pilger, so sheep were new to me. I liked these wooly creatures and often helped Grandpa feed them. One time, Grandpa was bent over a fence pouring water into a trough when a ram decided Grandpa's behind was a good target. I turned my head just in time to see the ram run across the pen and pitch Grandpa over the fence. He got up, dusted himself off and said, "Rats." That was the extent of Snyder profanity.

Another time, Dad took me with him to a livestock auction to buy some bred female sheep. He explained that they were called ewes. I got bored sitting in the stands waiting for Dad to bid on groups of ewes, so I wandered off and walked through the barns where sheep were kept in pens waiting to be auctioned. I came across a pen that had just one ewe. She was standing in the back, her sides heaving with labored breathing. I could see the fear in her eyes as she looked at me. I leaned on the gate watching her for a long time. No one was around, so I crawled over the gate and found a clean place to sit down. The ewe watched me with wary eyes, keeping her distance. After a while, to my surprise, she came over and laid down beside me.

Dad panicked when he realized I was gone. When he found me, I was sitting in the pen sleeping. The ewe was also asleep with her head on my lap. Relieved, Dad woke me, told me to wait there and that he would be right back. When he returned he said it was time to go home. As I got up he said to me, "And she is coming, too." It was early spring, and I named her Blossom. A month later she had a lamb. I named him Bud.

I was learning how to work but I didn't yet recognize love.

CHAPTER 8

Home Alone
1957

In 1957, when I was 12, Dad bought his brother Phil's farm near the small town of Bennet. We moved from the house on my grandparents' farm, east of Lincoln, to this new farm in early spring, and Karen and I transferred to the Bennet school—just two months before the end of the school year. Once again, I was the outsider in my classroom.

Though the new farm was less than 11 miles from our old place, I missed my grandparents, George and Lela Snyder. Grandma Snyder understood my loneliness when I moved from Pilger in 1953. I had often walked the quarter mile to her house in midafternoon to spend time with her. Our time together was always comforting. After we moved to the Bennet farm, I was happy Dad continued to farm Grandpa's 160 acres in addition to our new farm. When I drove the tractor to my grandparent's farm, I could stop by for a quick visit with Grandma and Grandpa before heading to the field.

Not only birthdays, but Christmas holidays which also focused on the youngest children, were difficult for me after I moved back to Dad's. After moving to Bennet, the Christmas holiday became even worse. Our family always spent a few days during Christmas at Percy's parents' home—they lived a couple hours west of Lincoln. When we lived on Grandpa Snyder's farm near Lincoln, Grandpa took care of the livestock while we were gone. Now that we lived in Bennet, someone else had to stay behind to look after the livestock. At 13, I was capable of doing the routine chores, caring for the hogs and sheep and milking our one cow, so I was the logical choice. Even though I wanted to be with the family, part of me looked forward to my first Christmas alone. A new adventure. I felt like an adult, with important responsibilities.

The days leading up to Christmas were festive and busy. Karen and Percy cooked holiday foods and wrapped presents. Dad organized the farm chores so I could take care of everything while they were gone. Tim and Reb got more and more excited to see Santa. On Christmas Eve, departure day, the house was a frenzy. Suitcases were packed, presents were gathered, food was assembled and the car was loaded. Everyone was eager to leave. Dad gave me his last instructions. Then they were off. I would be alone for three days, in charge of the farm.

I had not anticipated how being alone at Christmas would feel. The silence was stark. The house felt cold. I walked into the living room and looked at the Christmas tree, a spindly small-needle pine that Percy and Karen had decorated. It hadn't looked too bad with presents underneath. Now, with presents removed, it looked pathetic. In their rush to leave, my three gifts had been left on the dining room table, so I put them back under the tree. I knew what they were by their shapes. A shirt from Dad and Percy, a box of chocolates from Percy's parents and a box of Life Savers that opened like a book. The Life Savers were my annual Christmas gift from my mother's parents, Grandma and Granddad Nickens. I opened the shirt and the Life Savers. I decided to wait to open the chocolate covered cherries, so the enjoyment would be spread over the next two days. Percy had left portions of the pending Christmas dinner, but I didn't feel like eating. I sat in the living room for a long time, looking at the bleak Christmas tree. I thought about the rest of the family laughing and celebrating with grandparents, aunts and uncles and a loneliness that I had not felt since my first summer in the Turkey Shack returned.

It was cold outside and getting dark, so I decided to do the chores before it got even colder. Work might alleviate my deepening gloom, and my dog Pep would keep me company while I fed the livestock. After I finished the chores and shut off the one light in the barn, I was shocked at the total blackness of the starless night. I had not turned on a light in the house, and finding my way back was difficult. Pep, being a farm dog, was not allowed in the house, so I left him in his dog house with the heat lamp. Once inside the house, I was alone.

It was my first night by myself in the house, which had not worried me. I assumed my nights in the Turkey Shack had prepared me. Still, my mood worsened. We didn't have a television and I couldn't get interested in reading, so I just sat on the sofa. I got up and turned off the Christmas tree lights, which, for some reason, improved my mood. I still had no appetite, but I decided to eat one of the chocolate covered cherries. That helped so, I had another one and then another one. By the time I went to bed they were gone. Maybe that's why, to this day, I enjoy anything chocolate.

This alone-at-Christmas ritual continued for several years, until Tim and Reb were older and the family started to celebrate the holiday at home. I didn't discuss my Christmas loneliness with Dad. I assumed the best solution for taking care of the livestock was to leave me at home. Years later when we talked about it, Dad said, if he had known how I felt, he could have found someone else to do the livestock chores.

My inability to communicate continued to plague me.

CHAPTER 9

Truck Driving
1957-1958

When I first began spending my nights in the Turkey Shack, Dad was raising 10,000 turkeys each year. That number increased to more than 20,000 by the time I was a young teenager. We bought day-old turkeys called poults in the spring, then raised them until they were marketed in the fall. Turkey production was labor intensive, so by the end of each summer I was in great physical condition.

In addition to our farm near Bennet and Grandpa's farm near Lincoln, we now farmed Dad's 240-acre farm near Douglas, Nebraska, 23 miles southeast of our Bennet farm. This was the farm my dad retreated to after my mother's death. Much of the farm acreage was cropland, and we raised corn, grain sorghum, soybeans and wheat. I liked working crops and Dad preferred working with the livestock, so I spent many long days on a tractor. There were no enclosed, air-conditioned cabs in those days. I was out in the elements. My sweat mixed with the dust turned my face black, so when I washed up for lunch, my face became white, bordered by my black head. I laughed at my reflection because I looked like a monkey, but the dirt and sweat didn't bother me. I enjoyed the repetition of driving a tractor back-and-forth, back-and-forth, across a field. I took comfort in the tractor's rocking motion over uneven ground, and in the melodious sound of the engine. I often fell into a relaxed, contemplative state. Reflecting on those days, I now recognize my first foray into meditation was on a tractor.

But most of my daily chores were related to livestock. Sheep grazed our pastures, and hogs ate our grain. We had 150 to 200 ewes, plus their lambs, which we sold in the fall to farmers who raised them to market weight. Our hog numbers were small—10 to 12 sows that each produced two litters a year. We raised these pigs to market weight.

Dad and I became more accepting of each other, but most of our time together was spent working. Dad was not one to give excessive instructions. Our conversations were short. He explained what needed to be done and maybe the order in which to do it. Beyond that, I was on my own. For example, one of my summer responsibilities was mixing 20-30 tons of feed each week and delivering them to the growing flock of turkeys. Dad taught me how to mix the feed for the turkeys and other livestock, but he never checked up on me. Sometimes Dad helped me but, as was the case when we worked side-by-side on other jobs, we worked without conversation. He was not a man to joke around. No small talk. Ever. Just focus on the job at hand.

I now drove our 1951 Chevy 1-ton truck without assistance. I drove it to the field to deliver feed to the turkeys, then drove it back to the feed shed to mix more feed. I felt very grown up when Dad let me drive three miles to the grain elevator in the small town of Cheney, to get a load of cracked corn. I was 12, so it was an exciting expedition for a young boy without a driver's license. I didn't even mind when the elevator men teased me about my small size and my big truck. I was lucky I never had the embarrassment of driving into something.

When I was 13, Dad had me drive the truck seven miles to the nearby town of Roca to get cracked corn. This was a bigger adventure—not because of the distance but because of the hills. Driving the empty truck to Roca was no problem. Returning home with a full load of corn was another story. Our truck was old and the kingpins in the front axle were worn. As soon as I started down the steep hill outside of Roca, with two tons of corn on board, my speed increased, and the engine started to race. The loose steering and heavy load made the truck even harder to handle, so I swerved all over the road. Halfway down the hill I had to downshift to slow down, a tricky, dangerous operation because, I had to stretch to reach the clutch and gearshift while steering to keep the truck on the road. After the descent, the road climbed another steep hill, so near the bottom I shifted back into high gear and pushed the accelerator all the way to the floor to gain speed. This meant speeding over a narrow bridge while wrestling my heavy, wandering truck.

Once I crossed the bridge, I knew I had to downshift twice, or maybe three times, to climb the next hill. The Chevy's six-cylinder engine didn't have much power, so downshifting was necessary. My strategy on those first trips was to downshift early into first gear—the granny gear— (so named because your granny could walk faster) then creep up the hill with the engine roaring. I felt conspicuous and not very grown up roaring up the hill in low gear. I was just lucky I never had an accident on the road home from Roca. And I always made it to the top of that hill.

As I gained more experience, I could now shift gears when I needed to, and I could crest the hill in second gear never using granny. I no longer felt conspicuous. On warm days when the windows were down, I even placed my left arm on the windowsill just like the men did. Even though my elbow was as high as my head, I felt like a grown man.

Whenever Dad instructed me to get a load of corn, I hoped he would say from Cheney, not Roca. Maybe I should have told him how scared I was, but our pattern of not communicating was established. I said nothing. Dad never asked. He was always careful at work and he assumed I would be too, so he never thought I was in danger. Dad must have been right, because, in all the time I worked on the family's farms, we never had a serious injury or accident. I had learned to work quietly and do what it took to get the job done, like my dad and grandfather.

I was still young, but I could now work like a man.

Chevy truck like the one Dave drove   Pencil sketch by Don Greytak www.dongretak.com

CHAPTER 10

The Night in the Manger 1958

Even though Dad and I were both guilty of hiding our pain, I also learned from him how to endure pain. Livestock production in no way resembles the vision portrayed in books, such as Old McDonald's farm. Even though there is a relationship, even a bond, that develops between animals and their caretakers, it does not all take place on a sunny spring day. There are sub-zero days when water pipes freeze, tractors won't start, and animals just try to get enough feed and water to stay alive. Disease, loss and death are a very real part of life on the farm.

For example, thunder and lightning scare turkeys, causing them to run together and pile up, suffocating those underneath. I spent many hot, muggy summer mornings after violent thunderstorms picking up dead turkeys. Sometimes the losses eliminated all profits for the year, but Dad never complained. We picked up the dead turkeys and threw them into the truck to take them to the rendering plant. It was just part of raising livestock.

Lambing season, in late winter, was also difficult. Mother ewes needed help birthing their newborn. Dad spent hours, day and night, helping the ewes deliver their lambs, and orphan lambs depended on his personal attention for their survival. Obviously, Dad had a vested interest in the lambs' survival as they were a source of income. But he was always gentle and patient with the animals. He instilled in me the idea that we were caretakers, not masters. "Treat them with respect. They are in your care," he would say. That made a lasting impression on me. I also learned that animals may understand us better than we do them. I came to understand they can detect our moods and emotions.

I had a direct experience of this during the second Christmas I stayed home alone. Like the year before, my family left for Percy's parents' home on Christmas Eve. I thought this Christmas would be easier, now that I was 14. But the day they left was another cold, gray winter day.

As the afternoon progressed the temperature dropped and so did my spirits. I can still remember the clouds. They were low and dark, a steel-blue gray, and they limited my view, imprisoned me, compressed me and made me feel more alone. As I sat in the living room in the late afternoon, a howling wind hit the north side of the house, making it seem colder inside—so cold I checked the thermostat to make sure the furnace was working. It was.

As I had the year before, I decided to do the chores early hoping to finish before dark. I put on my coveralls, overshoes, cap, leather mittens and a heavy parka and headed out into the piercing wind with my dog, Pep. I milked the cow, checked the hogs to make sure they had feed and water, then fed the sheep. Normally they would get silage, but I couldn't get the tractor started in the cold, so I fed them hay and a small amount of grain. With their heavy wool coats, the sheep usually stayed outside in this kind of weather, even though they had access to shelter in the barn. But I decided to spread some straw in the barn, thinking that might entice them inside and out of the bitter cold. Besides, it was Christmas. I smiled as I thought they should be inside near the manger. Pep, who was an English shepherd and herded the sheep, stayed in the barn searching for mice and rats while I spread straw with a pitchfork. This was an added chore and by the time I was done making a *straw in the manger* bed for the sheep, it was dark.

Back inside the house I could not get warm. I was alone and bored, and it was still early in the evening. I sat down on the sofa and covered myself with a blanket. My mood continued to sink, just like the year before. After finding no way to overcome my despair, I headed upstairs to bed, but I was still chilled, even under extra blankets. I tossed and turned for what seemed like hours. Just past midnight, I decided to get up and see whether the sheep had availed themselves of my gift of straw.

When I stepped outside, Pep emerged from his dog house, surprised but excited to see me. We headed to the barn. The wind had died down, and the crunch of my boots on the snow was deafening compared with the utter silence of the cold night. I strained my eyes in the dark to see if any sheep were outside. I saw none. They must all be inside. My manger idea must have worked. I opened the barn door, reached for the string and turned on the single light-bulb. All the sheep were in the barn. Every one of them was lying down. Pep came in beside me and I closed the barn door behind us. The sheep typically moved away when Pep was with me because he was the herd dog. Not this time. As I stood and watched the sheep lying in the straw, most of the sheep raised their heads and looked at me. Although the door to the outside pen was open, not a single sheep moved.

A wave of loneliness overcame me, and I began to cry. Pep pushed against my leg and whined, perhaps wondering what was happening. I did not want to return to the cold empty house, so I sat down by the door. But there was a cold draft on my back and I saw a pathway to the middle of the flock, where it looked warmer. I crawled through the sheep, with Pep following. I could tell some sheep were more alert than others, but still none of them moved. When Pep and I reached the middle of the flock, I lay down on the straw and pulled my parka around my face. Pep nestled against my chest and I held him close to me. We were as close to the sheep as they were to each other. My last thought before I fell asleep was, this was my Christmas night in the manger, which brought a faint smile to my lips.

I awoke at daybreak to the sound of milling sheep. Pep was still lying beside me but many of the sheep had gone outside. I was rested. My gloom was gone. Had the sheep sensed my loneliness and my need for comfort? Had they felt my pain? I began to think there might be more to life than I understood. As an adult, when I began to have other experiences that I could not explain, I often recalled that night in the barn with the sheep.

I also wondered whether Dad had found similar comfort from the animals he cared for, as he healed from the pain of my mother's early death.

But I never asked, and I never told him about my night in the manger.

Dave with his three Southdown sheep and little Tim and Reb at Lancaster County Fair

CHAPTER 11

I Can Take Care of Myself
1962

Aconversation I had with my mother shortly before she died remains vivid in my mind, even though I was only twenty-two months old when it happened. She took me onto her lap and gently held my head, so I was looking into her eyes. She said she was sorry but she had to leave, and I must take care of myself. She then held me to her chest for a long time. I remember pushing back and telling her I didn't want her to go, but if she must I could and would take care of myself. There were tears in her eyes but none in mine. I was not angry. I was resolute.

This memory has been with me since I was a small child in Pilger, and it's as real to me today as it was then. Did it happen that way? Most people would say it did not, given my age. But years later, Dad told Karen and me that just before our mother died she had asked to see each of us separately. He also reminded me that I was talking in complete sentences at that age. So maybe the gist of the conversation was real. And if it was a dream I had later, it was so vivid that it seemed real. I now know there is a reality beyond our physical existence. Perhaps the conversation came from there. The idea that stuck with me was simple: I can and will take care of myself. This thought guided me for decades, both to my benefit and my detriment. Throughout my childhood, I never escaped feel-

47

ings of estrangement from Dad and the rest of my family. I took refuge in my self-sufficiency. I didn't need help from others. That remained my approach to life until another unexplainable event occurred nearly 48 years after that conversation with my mother.

But, as a teenager, I was self-reliant. I was not a reclusive introvert. I was interested in girls, sports and school—in that order. I was outgoing and a joker—sometimes even a showoff, probably as a reaction to my quiet life at home. And as Tim and Reb grew older, Karen and I felt more included in the family, mainly thanks to Percy. She became more comfortable being a mother to all four of us. She was also much more social and outgoing than Dad.

I played basketball in junior high and high school, but my favorite sport was football. Dad allowed me to play football as a freshman and sophomore at Bennet, but only if it didn't interfere with my chores. He thought sports were a waste of time. My freshman year, I wasn't old enough to drive but Dad refused to take me to practices or games. I had to finish my chores, then walk three quarters of a mile, carrying my football gear in a duffle bag to the next county road intersection, where I got a ride with neighbors. If chores took too long, I had to run so the neighbors didn't have to wait.

During my sophomore year we had a good football team. We were undefeated and won most of our games by large margins. After home games, a local men's club served chili to players and fans, and the women served dessert. It was a community celebration, and as a running back I got a lot of attention. But Dad and Percy never came to a game or the chili supper, nor would Dad talk about games at home. He never asked who won. I'd come home and go to bed. No discussion.

In one game, I scored four or five touchdowns, thanks to our great offensive line, and I was named state Player of the Week in one of the major newspapers in Nebraska. I found out about it in school but said nothing when I got home. The next day our neighbor Mildred came over with the paper to congratulate me. Percy read the article and was effusive in her praise. Then she handed the story to Dad. He wouldn't even look at it. After Mildred left, I took another of my many long walks alone in the pasture. By this time in my life walking alone had become my solace. Dad and I didn't talk about this event until much later in our lives. The conversation was brief. He never explained his lack of interest in my achievement and it remained a painful memory that never healed.

Dad and I also had a falling out when he wanted me to transfer to University High School in Lincoln after my sophomore year. The school was on the University of Nebraska campus. Academically, it was one of the best high schools in the state. Dad wanted me to go there because University High offered opportunities unavailable at a small school like Bennet. But I didn't want to leave my friends in Bennet, and I did not want to give up football, which University High did not offer. But my arguments failed, and I transferred to my fourth school system.

As I describe my dad's reaction to my short football career more than 50 years later, I realize I might sound too critical. I know he wanted the best for me, and there were two times he expressed approval. One was when I was accepted into the American Field Service exchange program to spend the summer between my junior and senior years living with a farm family in Sweden. As I boarded the bus to leave home, he hugged me and there were tears in his eyes. The second time was when I gave the commencement address when I graduated from University High School. Again, I noticed there were tears in his eyes when I finished my speech.

I still wished Dad had watched me score a touchdown, but later in life I realized he was teaching me to take care of myself the same way he had learned. My aunts told me how they watched my dad, as a little 8-year-old boy, sitting on the disk behind four draft horses the size of Clydesdales. Because of his small size and the dust behind the horses, they could hardly see him. He had grown up in an age when work was more important than play.

I graduated from high school knowing I could take care of myself.

But I still could not feel love from my dad.

David Snyder, Lancaster county farm youth, is headed for Sweden this week where he will study European agricultural techniques. (SUN Staff Photo)

CHAPTER 12

The Calf is Weaned
1963

S hortly after I graduated from high school, Dad sat down with me at the kitchen table. "Well, you're going to college, so you need to get a summer job," he said. It was one of Dad's rare directives. I wanted to study agriculture at the University of Nebraska, so I asked if he would help pay for it. He said no. I reminded him that he helped Karen. Why not me? "She needed my help," he said. "You don't. You can work your way through college." End of conversation.

I knew Dad was confident I could take care of myself. I knew I could too, but I also felt I was being pushed out of the nest with no support. I felt abandoned once again. I accepted his decision without argument—perhaps to prove to him that I didn't need his help. I left the kitchen and headed to the pasture at the far end of the farm. As I walked I recognized that in one short conversation, the calf was weaned.

I found a summer job sampling grain in railroad boxcars for the Nebraska Wheat Commission. It was hard physical work and I sweat a lot, but the pay was good. By fall, I was in the best physical condition of my life and I had saved a considerable amount of money for college.

Because they were on the same campus, my two years at University High School facilitated my transition to college at the University of Nebraska. With help from my high school counselor I applied to college, registered for classes and found lodging in a dormitory. Neither Dad or Percy were involved in the process. In September, I moved into the dormitory by myself. Other students were being helped by parents and siblings. Once again, I felt alone. My new roommate arrived with his family and I remember helping unload boxes from his older brother's maroon 1962 Pontiac Grand Prix. I was envious of the beautiful new car. I had a faded, rusted 1949 Plymouth that I had parked in the far end of the parking lot, so no one would see it.

The day I moved into the dormitory was a warm, sunny, early September day, so when my roommate and his family went to dinner, I decided to explore the Ag campus which was new to me. A walk might dispel my loneliness. I started out on sidewalks and immediately noticed a difference. At home I walked in fields. Tilled fields always felt better than grass and much better than concrete. On sidewalks, the world seemed different. I walked east until I reached the buildings on the far edge of the campus. Beyond were crops, which beckoned me. I continued walking through fields of soybeans and corn that I later learned were agronomy research plots. I felt revived. I was home again.

As a freshman, I had a work-study scholarship and was assigned to the hotel at the Nebraska Center for Continuing Education. I worked there as a desk clerk. My sophomore year, I was the night manager and night auditor. I was dorm counselor my junior and senior years, which paid my board and room. I always took a full course load, and I was also active in student government. At the same time, I enjoyed an active social life. I had learned how to work hard on the farm. Now I was working and, at the same time, enjoying college.

After I finished my undergraduate studies I decided to enroll in law school. I talked Dad and Grandpa into letting me raise turkeys as a summer job before entering law school in the fall. Grandpa was retired, so he let me use his vacant facilities rent free. Dad financed the operation. Near the end of my undergraduate senior year, I prepared grandpa's dilapidated barns and old equipment for the arrival of my day-old-poults—all 8,000 of them. It was a new adventure and I expected it would pay much better than any other summer job.

I cared for my turkeys all summer while I lived in my grandparent's basement. All was well. When I started law school, however, I took a position as assistant residence director of a 500-man dormitory—another fulltime job in addition to raising 8,000 turkeys and, of course, going to law school. My routine was brutal. I got up early and drove to Grandpa's farm for turkey chores, then returned to the dorm to clean up and bicycle to class, which lasted until 4 p.m. I then worked at the dorm until 9 p.m. after which I returned to the farm for turkey chores in the dark. I couldn't keep up.

Then the fall weather turned cold and wet, and the processing plant couldn't take my mature turkeys until early December. Due to the freezing weather and my inadequate care, the turkeys lost weight. After they went to market, I turned the checks over to Dad. I had made nothing, and I'm certain Dad lost money. I don't know for sure because, like most difficult subjects, we never talked about it. He never expressed any displeasure, either. That was just the way it was.

One spring day near the end of my first year of law school, the classroom windows were open. The lawn was being mowed. I inhaled the smell of the fresh mowed grass and instantly realized I wanted to sit on a tractor, not behind a desk. Just as quickly as I had decided to enroll in law school, I decided to quit. I closed the book on my desk and never studied for the remainder of the semester. I finished my first year and passed, but I didn't return. Instead, I went on to earn a master's degree in agricultural economics.

Despite the turkey fiasco, I more than survived my seven years in college. I earned bachelor's and master's degrees and left school with one outstanding loan for $500. Dad was right. I could do it on my own.

There was one major decision where I could have used some parental guidance. After law school, I married Ann Albers. In the months leading up to the wedding, I realized it would be a mistake for me. As was my practice, I said nothing. As the day drew closer and everyone was busy with wedding plans, it became harder to say no. My future bride was a wonderful person and my family seemed pleased but when the wedding day arrived, I stood at the altar with sweat running down the back of my neck. I wanted to run but didn't.

I was married, but scared, for I felt no love.

CHAPTER 13

Grandma's Wisdom
1973

In the spring of 1971 I was euphoric. After seven years of college and a stint in the U.S. Army, I was ready to start a career in farming. Confinement hog production was the next big thing in agriculture. It was management intensive, and I saw myself as a successful manager. Though still a young man, I had experienced raising hogs as a teenager. Now I was college educated, and I was filled with a naïve belief in my ability to succeed. I knew I could make a lot of money, and I had a plan.

My uncle Larry, who lived near us, wanted to raise feeder pigs, so we concocted a loosely conceived joint venture. I would own the breeding herd and raise the piglets to eight weeks of age, at which point I would sell them to Larry. He, in turn, would feed them to market weight. Dad agreed to let me use land on his farm, rent free, for my portion of the venture. I would need money to construct the facilities, buy the animals to breed and have an operating line of credit. Since I had no business experience or collateral, Dad co-signed a loan from the local Production Credit Association to finance the venture. My plan was to begin with one hundred unbred female hogs, called "gilts." I needed one building to house the gestating gilts, and another for the sows to give birth and nurse the newborn piglets. I also needed buildings and pens to house the pigs from the time of weaning until I sold them to my uncle.

Although I didn't really know what I was doing, or even how to begin, somehow, I built the facilities myself. My sweat equity saved a lot of money, but the finished facilities were very poor quality. Nevertheless, the gilts arrived and were bred. Everything was good, or so I thought. I sat with the first gilt as she began to deliver. Normal litters have eight to ten pigs. My first litter had two. Very disappointing. Soon I discovered that all my gilts had uterine infections—their litters averaged just three pigs. I had to repopulate the breeding herd and start over. Dad accompanied me to the Production Credit Association to meet with my loan officer. I was uncomfortable, but Dad was calm. He had experienced other farming losses. The loan officer too, was understanding. He increased and extended my line of credit. New gilts arrived and were bred. But the new herd had the same problem. The litters averaged five piglets. I was devastated. Ann and I were expecting our first child, and we were broke. We were living rent free in an old farmhouse on Dad's farm, but where would the money come from to pay for living expenses and the upcoming medical costs? Dad had co-signed my note. He could pay it off and I could pay him back, eventually, but that didn't seem right to me. I continued to care for the hogs as I tried to figure a way out of an impossible situation. I had failed again—first turkeys and now hogs. How could I have let this happen? Was agriculture, which I loved, the wrong profession for me? I slipped into depression.

At my lowest point, Grandma Snyder invited me over for iced tea and cherry pie á la mode—my favorite. We made small talk, then she got down to business. She knew I was depressed, but her opinion about my situation took me aback. "This is the best thing that will ever happen to you," she said. What? My world was shattered. Had she no sympathy? I was speechless! After the silence, she proceeded to tell me a story about farming with Grandpa in the

1920s. They had a large, profitable farming operation, so in 1928 Grandpa borrowed money to buy his mother's farm. In the same year, he built a new two-story brick home for their large family. "You know about the stock market crash of 1929?" Grandma asked. Of course I did. And I knew it was followed by severe drought, low to zero crop production, unimaginably low commodity prices and a severe economic depression. "We lost everything," Grandma said. I was starting to feel a little ashamed of my own despair. "What happened?" I asked. "Grandpa was a quiet man, like your Dad," Grandma said. "He never blamed anyone else for his troubles. Grandpa always said he could lose everything but his integrity, and it was true." She explained he started over, renting foreclosed farmland from bankers who knew they could trust him. "If you can maintain your integrity, you still have your most important asset. That is the lesson you can learn as well as learning that you can survive failure," Grandma told me. "The choice is yours, Dave."

I returned home and fed the hogs. When I was finished, I walked across the pasture to sit by the farm pond, one of my favorite places of solace. I thought about my conversation with Grandma, and as I watched the water ripples on the surface of the pond, I knew with absolute certainty what I was going to do. For the first time in many months I felt a lightness in my mood. As I returned to the house, my steps were buoyant. I heard the birds and cicadas, smelled the damp grass and watched a magnificent sunset. I was back with the living.

The next morning I went to visit my loan officer at the Production Credit Association—alone. I thanked him for his help and the confidence he had placed in me. I told him I was going to close my hog operation. I would sell the hogs and equipment and apply the money to the loan balance. The sale of the assets wouldn't pay off the loan. I knew the bank had the right to collect the balance from Dad, but I asked him to not do that and convert what I owed to a seven-year personal loan. With a master's degree in agriculture, I was confident I could get a job and pay off the debt. The loan officer looked at me in silence for a long time. Then he leaned back in his chair and said, "OK."

My problems were not solved. Our baby was due in a month. I had no way to pay the upcoming medical bills. I had no job and no immediate prospects. But soon our beautiful daughter Carly was born, and shortly thereafter I was hired as a farm manager by a company in Columbus, Nebraska. Through a combination of salary, bonuses, land investments and profits from buying and selling houses, I paid off the loan in three years.

I knew the cleanup of my defunct hog facilities was my responsibility, but I now lived over 100 miles away and I never got around to the cleanup. The sight of the abandoned buildings bothered me whenever I visited Dad and Percy. A few years later when I drove past the site, to my amazement, the buildings were gone, and the land had been returned to crops. Sheepishly, I told Dad I'd reimburse him for the cleanup expenses. "It's OK," he said. "No need to pay me."

Grandma Snyder was right. Learning to keep my integrity, and realize I was strong enough to survive failure were invaluable lessons. If I had paid closer attention, I might also have understood how much my dad loved me.

I wouldn't understand that love until much later in life.

CHAPTER 14

A Business Born in a Blizzard
1976

In 1976, with my hog debt paid in full, I was ready for a new adventure. I had become good friends with Dave Luers, who worked for the local alfalfa dehydrator in Columbus, Nebraska. In late summer during our morning coffee get-togethers, we developed a plan to start our own farming and farm management business. I was 31 and Dave was 28. Our exuberance for the new business idea masked our naïveté and lack of financial resources.

Our business plan was quite simple. We'd both find a way to work for a year without a salary. Then we would borrow money to buy the farming equipment. We'd buy just one tractor, which we'd operate 24 hours a day, each of us driving a 12-hour shift. That way we could farm twice the land, earn twice the income, and pay off the equipment loan at the end of the year. We had enough cash to buy a used three-quarter ton Dodge Power Wagon, thinking the big pickup truck would signal to potential clients that we were for real.

We did not have money for a down payment on the tractor, but I knew three farmers who needed someone to dig re-use irrigation pits. The pits collected run-off irrigation water for recycling, and a government program, that ended at the end of the year, would pay for the excavations. If we could dig three pits before the end of the year, the money we earned would make the down payment on the 160-horsepower tractor we'd need for farming the next year, as well as the dirt excavating scraper we'd need to dig the pits. When the three farmers hired us, a local implement dealer sold us the new tractor and earth scraper on our promise to make the down payment within a month when the three pits were excavated.

We were in business! I had to wait until the end of the year to quit my farm management job. Dave was able to quit his job in the fall, so he was available to dig the three pits. Everything was going well—at first. (Sound familiar?) Dave was digging the second pit in early December when a winter storm barreled down on Nebraska. High winds, heavy snow and sub-zero temperatures were on the way. If we didn't start digging the third pit immediately, the ground would soon be frozen under two feet of snow and we wouldn't have enough money for the promised down payment on our machinery.

As the snow started and the wind became stronger, I left work to meet Dave at the second pit. There was only one solution. Dave would finish that pit by late afternoon while I took the pickup into town for diesel fuel. When I returned, we'd fuel the tractor, grease the scraper and I'd drive the tractor 10 miles to the third pit, on Max Gabel's farm. I would start digging before the blizzard hit. Once the pit was outlined and I knew where to pile the excavated dirt, I could continue digging through the night, despite the snowstorm. Our plan was for Dave to return in the morning, refuel the tractor and continue digging. He would finish by nightfall and we would have the money needed to start our new business.

When I returned with the diesel fuel, Dave had just finished the second pit, but it was already snowing hard and the temperature had dropped 20 degrees since I had left to get the diesel fuel. I headed toward the Gabel farm, driving the tractor into blinding snow and a northwest wind. I stopped at the farmstead to let Max know I was there.

"What the hell are you doing here in this blizzard?" he asked.

"I'm here to dig your pit," I said.

I could tell he thought I was kidding, so I explained my plan. Now he thought I had gone mad. He told me what I already knew—the temperature was supposed to hit 20 below zero. I nodded and continued to explain, "If I make uninterrupted passes over the ground, I can continue digging before the newly exposed ground freezes. And if I don't dig the pit tonight, you won't get the government check." That got his attention. He smiled and shrugged. "Good luck," he said as he closed the door.

I got back into the tractor cab and turned the heater to high. I found the pit markers, scraped dirt around the perimeter, and made a place to dump the excavated dirt. This just might work, I thought, as daylight turned to darkness. As soon as it got dark, I got a surprise. I was excavating moist, warm dirt. When it was exposed to the bitter cold air, the result was fog, which, combined with blowing snow, reduced my visibility to near zero.

The pit was rectangular—about 250 yards by 100 yards. It was supposed to slope down from the edges to a center depth of 12 feet, which would not be hard to dig in daylight but with the reduced visibility, it bordered on impossible. I had never operated a dirt scraper and the ground was wet, making it difficult to develop a feel for the depth of cut. The fog also made it hard to tell when the scraper box was full. But I continued, round after round, until I slowly became more competent. After I developed a routine, the excavating became more intuitive with each repetition. My process was:

- Enter the pit and shift down to second gear.
- Open the throttle and lower the scraper blade.
- When the scraper is half full, push the button on the floor with my foot, which puts the tractor in second gear-low range.

- Continue filling until the tractor engine begins to pull down indicating the scraper is full.
- Raise the scraper blade, foot shift to high range and exit the pit at full throttle.
- Shift up to third gear and drive to the dirt pile to dump.

Hour after hour I continued, all the while trying to keep the cab's windows defrosted. Miraculously, I kept ahead of the frozen ground. I even started to relax and enjoy myself, driving the first tractor I ever owned. Not only was it new but it was larger than any tractor I had ever driven. I began dreaming of farming next spring.

In the middle of the night I needed a bathroom break, and it was time to grease the scraper. I got out of the tractor cab. My God it was cold! I got the grease gun off the tractor, but frozen dirt encrusted the fitting on the first bearing. I tried to chip it off with the only tool I had that could possibly work—a very small screwdriver. No luck. Next bearing, same story. And the next. So, I gave up. Dave would have better tools in the morning. I returned to the warmth of the cab and continued through the night. The fog got worse and my progress seemed to slow. I had trouble staying awake and hoped morning would arrive soon.

Dave arrived at daybreak, not a moment too soon. He reported it was 19 below when he left town. That sounded about right to me. He had a big screwdriver and a hammer that took care of the frozen grease fittings. He told me to get into the warm pickup while he greased the scraper. He had hot coffee for me.

A couple minutes later he knocked on the truck window. He was laughing and motioned to me to come see something. He pointed to the scraper. Almost one-half of the scraper box was packed with frozen dirt. I had been taking out one half load at a time, which explained my decreasing production. We spent the next hour alternating with each other, chipping at the frozen dirt and warming up in the truck.

By now the snow and wind had abated. I went home to sleep. Dave finished the pit late that afternoon. Max got his government check, and we earned enough money to make the down payment on our new tractor and scraper. That was the beginning of a wonderful business partnership between Dave and me. Less than four years later, we moved our business and families to Pierre, South Dakota.

I was one step closer to the land that would become Pathways Spiritual Sanctuary.

CHAPTER 15

Crying on the Tractor
1979

When I married Ann Albers in 1968, I knew there was nothing wrong with my new wife. She was, and still is, a wonderful person. I thought the marriage would please my family. Ann's background was rural and protestant. She was attractive and working on a college degree. She was a good choice.

But I did not love Ann, so, predictably, the first few years of our marriage were difficult. We discussed divorce but never followed through. Instead, we decided having children might help. Our first daughter, Carly, was born in our fifth year of marriage. Three years later, our daughter Jaime was born. Our focus was now on two cute, vivacious daughters who brought joy into our lives. Unfortunately, the lack of connection between Ann and me did not change. I thought it would be dishonest to tell Ann I loved her, so I didn't. And I don't recall a time she told me she loved me. She may have, but verbalizing love was not part of our daily life. I remained emotionally distant. I was living a lie. One night, during a 12-hour shift on a tractor, in a remote field in the Nebraska Sandhills, my anguish broke the surface.

In the late 1970s, Dave and I began farming increasingly large acreages of center-pivot irrigated land in the northeastern Sandhills region of Nebraska. These farms were more than 120 miles north-west of Columbus, where our office and homes were located. In fact, the farms weren't near any towns, which made communication a problem. We installed UHF radios in our vehicles and tractors, which enabled local communication. We also erected a hundred-foot tall repeater tower on one of the highest hills between our farms and Columbus. That setup enabled us to communicate with our base radio, which was at my house. Ann and I routinely talked on the radio late in the evening, both to say goodnight and for her to make sure I was all right, as I was working alone on a tractor in the middle of nowhere.

The night of my acute anguish followed a day of frustrating breakdowns. When I called Ann, I proceeded to tell her, non-stop, about all that had gone wrong and how we were behind schedule. I stopped venting and had the courtesy to ask how her day had been. She didn't respond but she keyed the mike on the radio so I could hear. She said nothing, but I could hear two little girls crying and coughing. It went on for a while, and then Ann spoke, "Need I say more? Goodnight." The radio went silent.

I continued driving in stunned silence, overwhelmed with guilt for not being there to support my wife and help take care of our sick little daughters. When I heard those cries on the radio, so far away, I felt the fatigue and loneliness in Ann's voice. She was trying so hard to handle everything, and she deserved more from me.

I slumped heavily into the seat of the tractor and opened the throttle, hoping the roar of the 350-horsepower Cummins diesel would drown out my thoughts. As the dust swirled in the headlights, tears began streaming down my cheeks. I could not stop crying, so I stopped the tractor and stepped out into the cold air of the early spring night. I started walking across the dark field, wishing I could just walk away and not come back. But finally, when the lights of the tractor were specks in the distance, I turned and walked back.

I sat in the back wheel well of the 12-ton tractor feeling ashamed, powerless and confused. I could not have been more disillusioned with myself. Even though my tractor, with its engine idling peacefully, was by my side like a comforting pet dog at my feet, I cried harder and longer than I had since childhood. I felt so alone in that pitch-dark night in the middle of the Sandhills of Nebraska.

When my crying subsided, I returned to the warmth of the tractor cab. Driving a tractor had always been meditative and calming for me. Perhaps it was the redundancy of driving back and forth across the field, the constant motion, the sound of the engine, the smell of diesel. Whatever it was, as I continued driving through the night, a calmness returned, and my anguish returned to its hidden cave.

The next day I returned to my normal life, still living a lie.

CHAPTER 16

South Dakota and Divorce
1980–1993

V iewed from the outside, Ann and I were living the American Dream. We attended church, participated in our daughters' school activities and took family vacations. During the first 20 years of our marriage, we built two houses together and remodeled two others. We were socially active with friends and extended family. The business Dave and I began in 1976, grew rapidly and was financially successful. But beneath it all, Ann and I were unhappy, and I was angry with my inability to love her.

I focused most of my attention on our growing business. In 1980 our company signed a contract with a landowner north of Pierre, South Dakota, to manage the development of his farm property with center-pivot irrigation and, once developed, farm and manage the property. When the irrigation development was completed there were 12,000 acres of farmland under irrigation making it one of the largest irrigated farms in the United States. This was a tremendous and exciting opportunity for us, and we moved our company and families to Pierre and no longer farmed or managed farms in Nebraska.

Due to the unprecedented high interest rates in the early 80s and the landowner's high leverage, he filed bankruptcy in 1984 and our contract was terminated. In one day, we lost 90 percent of our business. We were devastated. Fortunately, within a few months we were able to find other land to farm and manage. Within a couple of years, we were farming and/or managing farms in South Dakota, Montana and Nebraska, totaling almost 90,000 acres, much different than the 320-acre farm I grew up on in southeast Nebraska.

At the same time our farm management business was rapidly expanding, we entered large-scale hog production in Colorado. Had I not learned a lesson? But this time we were financially successful, and our hog production enterprise grew rapidly. By the mid-1990s, our company (D & D Farms, Inc.) had 22,000 sows producing hogs for market, much different than the 10 to 12 sows on our farm when I was a kid, and much different than the 100 sows I had in my first unsuccessful hog production venture.

But while our business flourished, my personal life continued to flounder.

In mid-September of 1993, Dad and Percy visited Ann and me at our Black Hills ranch. One morning Dad and I sat together on the patio in the warm sun, drinking coffee and looking out across the beautiful mountain meadow. "I love Percy," Dad said without taking his eyes off the meadow, "but there has never been a day in my life I have not thought about your mother." I turned and looked at him. Tears ran down his face, and I was overwhelmed with sadness and compassion for him. Dad was now an old man and I realized there was part of him I had never known. Nor could I comprehend the depth of his love for my mother.

I didn't speak but turned my eyes back to the meadow thinking of my mother. I longed to know the woman I would have called Mom, and I yearned for the kind of love she and Dad must have shared. Dad was 25 years older than me and I didn't want to be sitting on this patio 25 years in the future, crying, not out of love, but because I had not experienced love. At that moment, I knew I had to end my marriage. We finished our coffee in silence, engulfed in a shared sadness.

That afternoon Dad and I walked across the meadow, enjoying the fall colors. "Dad, I'm going to ask Ann for a divorce." Then I asked him. "Do I have your support?" His response surprised me. "Ann is a wonderful woman, but I've known since before you were married that you were not right for each other." I asked, "Why didn't you say anything." He replied, "Percy and I thought it was none of our business."

But it was their business. They were my parents. As I thought this over, I recalled that at the time Ann and I married, I had already been weaned for several years.

In a month I would be 49 years old. It had been four decades since I faced my fears in the Turkey Shack. Now I would have to face fear again. On the ride home to Pierre, I stifled my fears and asked Ann for a divorce. To my surprise she agreed.

One of my overpowering fears about divorce was losing my daughters. After buying the Black Hills ranch in February 1993, Carly and Jaime spent most of that summer helping me build the first new building—a three-stall garage with an apartment on one end. Carly was 19 and would be a junior at Augustana College in Sioux Falls. Jaime was 16 and would start her senior year in high school. I enjoyed teaching them to hang drywall, install plumbing and pull electrical wiring. We worked together clearing the farmstead of junk and debris. Now, a month later, I would leave them. How could I handle their pain and probable anger?

Despite my fears, I knew I made the right decision. We filed for divorce, and I moved out of our beautiful house in Pierre, overlooking the Missouri River. The only furnished apartment I could find was an old garage that had been converted into an apartment, but I thought it was all I needed. When Carly and Jaime first visited, they started crying because they were dismayed about my living in such an ugly old apartment. Trying my best to cheer them up I said, "It's not as bad as the Turkey Shack!" My attempt at humor was not appreciated, and it didn't lighten their moods. My garage hovel with its musty smell was contributing to my growing depression.

I was engulfed in guilt and wanted the divorce to be as easy as possible for Ann and the girls. Ann chose to stay in the house until Jaime graduated from high school in June. But she didn't want to live there afterward, so we bought a new condominium that was under construction. She would move to the condominium after Jaime graduated. In January, when the condo was finished, I moved from the garage into the condo and lived there until Ann moved out of the house in June, (which I kept as part of the divorce settlement.) Moving from the musty garage into the sparsely furnished condo did not improve my mood. It smelled of new paint and felt more like a construction site than a home.

Guilt, anger and shame accompanied my thoughts about my uncertain future. These thoughts played in my head like continuous recordings. I missed my daughters—I was sure they blamed me for the divorce. My depression made it difficult to concentrate at work. Alone at the condo I was either listless or agitated. When I tried to read a book, my eyes scanned the words, but I had no comprehension of what I read. I couldn't focus enough to watch television. I spiraled deeper and deeper into despair. At the heart of my pain, there was always a question.

Why had I never learned to love?

Dave's parents Geneva and Wayne obviously in love

PART II—AWAKENING TO LOVE

CHAPTER 17

You Are Loved
1994

Walking has always been my solace. I knew I was in trouble when even that wouldn't ease my anguish after the divorce. Late one night on a walk in Pierre, I saw my reflection in a storefront window. I was 49, but the man in the window was hunched over and shuffling. For an instant I thought it was someone else. Startled, I straightened up and tried to pick up my pace. It didn't help. I continued to shuffle.

Over the past months, I had continued to decline into a deepening depression. The only relief I could find was in the positive energy at our office, but even there I was wearing a mask. Why didn't I seek professional help? My answer is a poor one. I had always kept my feelings to myself—just like Dad and my other male role models. Men don't go to therapy. Men are made to strut like the male turkey. Men don't cry like a baby.

When my lower back started hurting and my heart rate was abnormally high, I saw my family doctor. An X-ray showed my spine was curved to the left. The doctor attributed it to tight muscles caused by stress. He prescribed a muscle relaxant. He also told me my stress caused my elevated heart rate. But it wasn't high enough to be dangerous, so I didn't get medication for it. The morning after my appointment my back felt worse. In the bathroom mirror,

I saw a very large bruise on the lower left side of my back. I had no idea how I got it.

For months my sleep was sporadic. I was exhausted. It was Friday, and I decided not to go to work, thinking a long weekend would help me deal with my pain. Most of that day and evening I sat on the sofa, trying to watch television or read, but I still couldn't concentrate. I had no appetite. In the evening, I put on the heart-rate monitor I used when bicycling. The rate varied between 85 and 110 beats per minute—much higher than my normal resting heart rate of 65 beats per minute. I spent the rest of the evening trying to use my mind to lower my heart rate. It didn't work. Exhausted, I went to bed. As I lay on my left side, I could not quiet the recurring thoughts of guilt, shame and anger that were spinning in my head.

After a few minutes, my body started to slowly contract into the fetal position. I could not stop it. It coiled itself tighter and tighter into a ball. My fingers clenched into fists, my fingernails digging into the palms of my hands. I tried to open my hands but couldn't. I tried to straighten my legs but couldn't. I lay there paralyzed. It was like a whole-body cramp but without the pain. I was one big, knotted muscle. I was powerless, unable to move. I panicked! My heart was racing. Could I be dead?

Then I realized my eyes had locked shut. I focused on opening them and eventually felt them begin to open—but only enough to see a small crack of light. I could see the dim outline of the door to the bathroom. Maybe I wasn't dead. I tried to cry for help, but I couldn't speak. I could only think the words: "Help! Someone help me!" I kept repeating these words in my mind as I grew more fearful. Exhausted, I resigned myself to my paralysis. My eyes closed. Abruptly, I noticed the room was deathly quiet. The spinning thoughts in my mind had stopped. I must be dead! And then, in that profound silence, I heard three words: "You are loved." The words were soft, and gentle and kind. I thought, "What?" I heard them again. "You are loved."

And that was it. Nothing more.

I don't know how long I lay there with the three words echoing in my head. Were they words? Were they thoughts? Where did they come from? Was it a voice? I had no answers, but the thought that I was loved would not go away. My muscles began to relax. I could move my neck. My fingers uncurled. My legs began to straighten. I continued to sense the three words as tension left my body. The negative, recurring thoughts that had been in my head were silent and I passed into a deep, relaxed sleep.

When I awoke it was mid-day. I rolled over in bed and noticed my back didn't hurt. In the bathroom, I inspected my bruise. It was still there, but it went away in a couple of days. I checked my pulse. It was 65. I was rested.

My paralysis of the night before had been my first experience of *not* being able to take care of myself. My helplessness and the three-word message of my being loved, changed the perception of who I was. I realized I was not alone. I realized I could ask for help. Beginning that morning, I began to emerge from my depression. The three words *you are loved* not only helped me heal, they opened my mind and heart to the realization our reality extends beyond our physical experience. I didn't know how profound that realization would be.

My life was changed forever.

CHAPTER 18

Confusion
1994

As had been my lifelong experience, my refuge was the land. Over the next few months I spent almost every weekend at the ranch. I'd leave Pierre after work on Friday afternoon, drive the two hundred miles to the ranch and return to Pierre early Monday morning.

At the ranch I spent most days walking the 200 acres and much of the national forest surrounding it. I felt connected to it, embraced by it, comforted by it. Eventually, I was healed by it. I relished the solitude but never felt alone. I returned from those weekends with a lighter heart, and each visit lifted me one step further out of my depression.

The words *you are loved* confused me. My days walking at the ranch provided an opportunity to seek an understanding of what I had experienced. I am a predominately left-brained, logical male. I needed answers.

Although my *you are loved* experience was a rebirth of sorts, it also created anxiety as I contemplated the premise that I had spiraled downward, from a deep depression into a state of hearing voices. This had to be a sign of further psychological decline. But was it a voice? Or perhaps just a thought? If it was a voice, where did it come from? Whose voice? Mine? God? My mother? If it was my thought, why was it so different from my other thoughts of guilt, shame and anger? Why did those three words *you are loved* have such a physical impact on my body? Was my desperate plea for help a prayer and were the three words an answer to that prayer?

As I walked the land, thoughts continued to emerge that were of the same tone as the *you are loved* voice. I began to pay attention. They were gentle—almost a whisper—and always affirmative. They created a sense of calm and peace within me. I continued to try and determine their origin. Was this my voice? Was it male? Was it female? I could not tell, but it seemed to be none of the above.

Late one night I was driving on Highway 34 from Pierre to the ranch. From out of nowhere, I heard a very calm voice say, "Slow down." I was about to crest a hill, so I tapped my brakes to disengage the cruise control. Just over the top of the hill, a large herd of antelope sprinted across the highway. If I hadn't slowed down, there is no doubt I would have crashed into many of them.

What was it that warned me? Was it a voice? Maybe I just thought I should slow down. Maybe I just felt I should slow down. Maybe I had a gut feeling that danger was over the hill. But, it was precognitive which defied my understanding of time. Whatever I had experienced, it was protective and the same tone as the *you are loved* voice.

While walking at the ranch one afternoon, I recognized I was not only listening to the voice, I was having conversations with it. This scared me. Now I *had* gone over the edge. Not only was I talking to myself, but I was answering my own questions. Was I becoming schizophrenic? Is paranoia next? Or maybe I was hearing the whisper of an angel, or the voice of God. I did not know.

To ease my distress, I decided to just call what I was hearing a voice, at least something other than myself. But I was not going to tell anyone I was hearing voices! Once I came to terms with the description as a voice, a mental block was removed. My ability to listen and engage improved. The voice was, and still is, a descriptive word, not an explanation.

Once I opened myself to the voice thing, I moved into a new phase of curiosity, and the dialogues became more frequent. As a left-brained, rational male I analyzed. I could always differentiate this voice from other ruminations tumbling around in my head. The tone was always the same. It was never intrusive. The messages were short, concise, clear and loving—intercessions but not interventions. I was always in control. The voice felt unconditionally loving, even though I was not yet sure what that meant. It had no ego characteristics.

I was guilty of infidelity in our marriage. It was unethical, and it resulted in shame, guilt and anger that I carried hidden within me. After I filed for divorce, I made another mistake and I had a brief relationship with a married woman. I thought this relationship would resurrect me. Instead, it once again compromised my integrity and added to my anguish. It ended but the guilt remained.

If the voice I heard was the voice of God, why was there no judgement about these moral lapses? From my childhood religious teachings, I expected the voice to say: "Repent and then we will talk." Instead, the voice was always compassionate, loving and forgiving—never judgmental or damning. I was not witnessing a wrathful God. Never was there even a mention or insinuation of a Hell. But I want to be clear—I also had no feeling that my behavior was in any way condoned.

Although what I was experiencing didn't fit with my long-held religious beliefs of punishment and reward, it was consistent with the non-judgment and inclusiveness of the teachings of Jesus. My confusion and questioning continued.

I thought back to my teen years in the Turkey Shack. On warm and clear nights, I often delayed going into the shack to sleep. I would lie on the grass beside the shack, with Pep by my side, and gaze into the vast universe, focusing on the multitude of stars and the milky way. I marveled at how little I knew about our universe. The mystery of God was beyond my understanding and Bible stories had not helped my understanding. They were historical and abstract; not relevant to me. Now what was happening to me was experiential and personal. I was the one experiencing it, not some biblical story that happened thousands of years ago. It was happening now. Perhaps it wasn't real. Maybe it was my imagination. But no, it was real. Very real.

As a teenager, I assumed our Protestant church doctrines were correct, so by implication, others were wrong. When my sister Karen was a senior in high school, a classmate asked her on a date. Dad would not let her go because the boy was Catholic. I had just received our school class picture. I looked at it and wondered who in my class were the Catholics? And why were they a problem?

That question continued to plague me. Later, when I was attending University High School, I asked several of my fellow students where they went to church. I was surprised. They were Catholic, Methodist, Presbyterian, Lutheran and Episcopalian. There were two Jews. Many did not go to church at all.

These were my school mates. We were on the same basketball team. We served on student council together and we were in the same school plays. Until I asked their church affiliation, we had been one united student body. Now they had labels. How could we all have such different beliefs, or at the very least, different interpretations of the same Bible? My family had grape juice at communion. Those Catholics and Lutherans had wine. How decadent of them! It became apparent to me that what I and my classmates believed, was acquired from the beliefs of our parents. I ended my teenage years with the belief that our different religious backgrounds separated us more than brought us together.

During our marriage, religion did not play a large part in our personal lives. We went to church and participated in church activities, and many of our friends were from our church, but at home we did not read the Bible or pray together. In fact, religion and spirituality were never discussed in our marriage. We were members of the Lutheran Church, not because of careful introspection or choice, but for the simple reason that Ann was raised in a Lutheran home. I was Protestant because my family was Protestant. My beliefs were not grounded in a personal spiritual experience.

Now, after *you are loved*, I was intrigued and comforted by the fact that what I experienced was beyond my religious instruction. The voice I heard was always inclusive and there was never any reference to religious teaching, dogma or rituals. And yet, my experiences seemed to be at the heart of what religions intended to instill—spiritual guidance and assistance.

The analytical part of me was still confused. What were these intercessions and who, if anyone, was on the other end of the line?

I still did not know.

CHAPTER 19

The Awakening
1994–1995

Other than conversations with my daughters and occasionally with Dad and Percy, I discussed my voices with only a few close friends. As I wrestled with the reality of my experiences, I frequently confided in my daughters. Contrary to my fears, Carly and Jaime were understanding. I was grateful for their support, love and acceptance. Our conversations were reassuring.

I looked for affirmation of what I was experiencing in books and was relieved to discover that what I called intercessions were common human experiences. They'd been recorded throughout history and they had happened to people of all races, cultures, genders, religions and ages. Continuing to be the left-brained, logical guy, I also remained analytical. But I could not find conclusive, verifiable explanations for the phenomena. I could not find a why or how. My investigations most often ended with the word spiritual—defined as that which neither science or our five senses could explain. I resisted using the word at first. Spiritual had religious connotations, and I didn't want to be restricted by my religious belief system which, to me, was historical and not experiential. I relented, however, because spiritual—like hearing voices—was the easiest way for me to explain otherwise inexplicable events.

My experiences were becoming more frequent and varied. In January 1995, I attended a pork producers' convention on Marco Island in Florida. On the last night of the convention, I skipped the banquet. I was reading in my hotel room when I felt compelled to drive to a Barnes & Noble bookstore in nearby Naples. I didn't know what book I was going to buy, but I knew I would know it when I saw it. I had received directives like this several times since *you are loved*, so I paid attention. I didn't know where the bookstore was, but I just started driving, in the dark, through a rainstorm. When I pulled into the parking lot, I sat there for a moment. I hadn't asked for directions. I hadn't followed a sign. I couldn't even remember the route I took. But I was there. Inside, I walked directly to a shelf. My eyes focused on one book. I picked it up, looked at the front cover, read the back cover, bought it and returned to the hotel.

I crawled into bed and started to read *Opening to Channel* by Sanaya Roman and Duane Packer. The book described much of what had been happening to me since *you are loved*. One chapter described how to go into a deep meditative state. I decided to try it. I put a chair in the middle of the room, sat down, closed my eyes and began slow rhythmic breathing, as instructed. It was 11 p.m.

After a few minutes of focusing on my breath, a doorway appeared in front of me, outlined in white. A voice asked, "Do you want to go in?" I felt no fear, so I replied in the affirmative. "Are you sure?" I thought for a moment and said yes.

The door opened to the brightest, whitest light I had ever seen. Blurry figures were moving around. There were no voices or sounds. I was inside the door and I sat motionless, not interacting. I was just there. I felt as though I had merged with the experience surrounding me. The light was bright but there was a softness to it. It seemed to be engulfing and, despite the brightness, it was not blinding. Abruptly, I was back. I was sitting straight in my chair just as I had before I started meditating. I thought maybe a minute had passed. I looked at my watch. I had been sitting there for over an hour. I went to bed puzzled.

I awoke early, completely refreshed. I skipped the final morning lecture on hog nutrition and headed to the beach in shorts and a T-shirt, carrying my sandals. I felt strange. The best word to describe this feeling is light. I felt very light. I experienced a desire to run on the beach, though I had never been a runner. I clutched a sandal in each hand and took off at an easy pace, with consistent, methodical strides, like an accomplished runner. I was surprised I didn't tire. My heart rate remained steady. I ran and ran, until I reached the far end of the beach and back. By the time I stopped, I had run 3 miles, on sand, without exerting myself.

After the convention ended, I flew to New York City for a meeting. My lightness had not dissipated. On the early morning taxi ride to my meeting, I marveled at the brilliance of the colors; more vivid than my images during previous visits. The next day after returning to Pierre, during my customary noon racquetball game, I played at a higher level than ever before. One of my opponents asked, "What the hell is going on with you, Snyder?" I didn't know. Over the next few days my lightness, and the energy that came with it, dissipated. Could this be what some call a "spiritual experience"?

Another series of puzzling experiences began during the full moon on the night of September 30, 1993. I was in Oakland, California attending a national Rails-to-Trails Conservancy conference. The window in my hotel room faced west. I was awakened from a deep sleep at 4:30 a.m. I sat up in bed, and from where I sat, the setting moon was framed in the window. I thought: how strange that I awoke at the time the moon was in the center of the window. Several months later, I awoke again at the exact time the full moon was centered of the window in my bedroom at home. As I pondered this, it occurred to me I had seen every full moon since that late September night. As time went on I continued seeing every consecutive full moon. If it was cloudy, I would wake up at the exact time the moon was in a hole in the clouds, and then it would disappear. I kept track of these phenomena for 92 consecutive full moons. I sometimes asked myself: "Am I sane?" I still have no explanation for how this happened or why. I stopped paying attention to the experiences, and they stopped. I no longer wake up to witness every full moon, but I think I could if I needed to.

Another unusual phenomenon that I experienced relates to time. I began noticing that whenever my attention was drawn to a clock, the time suggested an arranged pattern. Either the same numbers such as 3:33 or consecutive numbers like 1:23. One night in 2003, when I was again feeling lonely and distressed, my familiar voice told me again that I was loved and suggested I should go to bed and get some rest. I got into bed and looked at the clock. It was 10:10 p.m. That felt comforting. I fell asleep, but awoke at 11:11 p.m., then again at 12:12 a.m. Despite the interrupted sleep, I felt better. I continued waking up in that pattern throughout the night—1:11 a.m., 2:22 a.m., 3:33 a.m., etc. In the morning, my despair was gone. I now know, from conversations with others and from reading books, seeing patterns of numbers like this is a common experience for many people. But how does the brain know when to awaken? Who is watching the clock? I don't know. Maybe there's a neurological explanation, but why did my experience leave me feeling calm and peaceful?

I had yet another kind of experience during this awakening period. It happened just once in my life. I told a few close friends about it, but since then I've read about many people having had similar experiences, so I feel more open to sharing it.

It happened one night in May 1994, in the light of a full moon. I sat on a hillside on the part of the ranch that would later become Pathways Spiritual Sanctuary. I looked down on the peaceful mountain meadow in the glow of the moonlight and thought about how sacred the land was to me. I felt connected to it. I had acquired it so easily. I asked myself: "Why am I here on this land?" Suddenly, I was surrounded by luminous beings. They appeared to be American Indian grandmothers. Eight of them stood in a circle around me. The one in front of me spoke. "You were chosen," she said. "For you will care for and protect this land." Then they were gone. Was this my imagination or a hallucination? Their appearance startled me, but it felt real. Her words took me back to the day I skied this land before purchasing it. It felt special, even sacred on that first day. The grandmothers' message reinforced that belief. Over the quarter-century that I have owned the ranch, I have always felt I was the caretaker and protector rather than the owner.

After the opening dedication ceremony of Pathways Spiritual Sanctuary on July 17, 2010, two people came to me, separately, and asked if I had seen the Indian warriors, in full regalia, riding horses along the far tree line during the ceremony. I smiled, remembering the grandmothers. I had not seen the warriors, but I believed those who had seen them. When I later asked others who had attended if they had seen the riders, they said they saw nothing.

I needed to talk with someone I trusted about my experiences. I was active in our Lutheran church, once serving as chairman of the building committee, so I knew the pastor well. I asked him to come to my house for a visit. We sat on the porch and I explained all that was happening to me, from the Grandmothers to the intercessions. I asked him to help me understand. He couldn't. In fact, he became very uncomfortable and soon left. In later conversations he never mentioned our visit.

His reaction triggered some doubts, but I knew what was happening was real. I came to accept that much of our reality cannot be explained by the cause-and-effect laws of science. The keys to my awakening had been awareness and acceptance. The three words *you are loved* had awakened me to a new reality.

I now accepted this new world as real.

CHAPTER 20

Prior Voices and Intercessions 1980s

I began wondering if these non-physical spiritual experiences were new to me, or if I had heard the voices or intercessions before? Perhaps I had but hadn't recognized them at the time. At least none were as awakening as the *you are loved* experience. I thought back to events that may have been precursors.

My unhappiness over my failing marriage frequently kept me awake at night. One sleepless night I tossed and turned for hours. I got up and went downstairs. I felt directed to find our Bible which was buried under a pile of books on a shelf. I opened it to a random page. A single verse caught my eye. I don't remember which verse, only that it was relevant. When I read it, I was amazed at the feeling of peace that washed over me. I went back to bed and fell into a deep sleep. Over the years I have often wondered what drew me to that verse on a random page, and how the words were the perfect antidote to my despair. I hadn't prayed, but I was drawn to the Bible, so perhaps there was a spiritual connection.

Another experience occurred in 1980 when the irrigation development began on the farm north of Pierre. We planted 5,000 acres of corn and soybeans, knowing the irrigation would not be ready for a month. Normal rainfall would be enough to germinate and grow the crops until we could apply irrigation water. But there was no rainfall that spring. After several weeks of no rain, we talked about disking the fields and re-planting a short-season crop, like oats or millet. One afternoon my partner Dave and I met with the landowner to inspect the fields and make our final decision. As we expected, most of the seeds were still lying in the dry dirt, ungerminated. No rain was forecast.

Replanting would be expensive, but it seemed we had no choice. We decided to disc the ground and plant millet. However, as soon as we agreed to a plan, I had a strong feeling we should delay our decision until morning. I thought it would rain. I remember looking to the west. The sky was clear. The air was hot and dry. There was no moisture in the soil, so we'd need at least two inches of slow rain, with no runoff, to save the crops. As the strong feeling was still with me, I asked Dave and the landowner to wait until morning to make a final decision. They disagreed, but we couldn't begin disking until the next day anyway. We would talk in the morning.

As I drove the 20 miles from the farm into Pierre, I kept looking west. There were no signs of rain. I watched the local weather that evening. No rain was forecast. When I went to bed that night, I prayed for rain. Just the right amount, with no runoff.

I awoke in the middle of the night to the sound of thunder, but the rain was only a sprinkle. Disappointed, I went back to sleep. The next morning I got an excited call from Dave, who lived on the farm. "We got 2½ inches last night! There was no runoff. Can you believe it?" I did believe it, but I didn't understand how it had happened. Was it the answer to my prayer? But my powerful thought that we should delay our decision had come many hours before my prayer.

Four years later, in early 1984, that same farm north of Pierre was in financial trouble. When the landowner filed Chapter 11 bankruptcy we lost our farming and management contract. We had given up all our farming operations in Nebraska when we moved to South Dakota, and this contract provided 90 percent of our income. Even worse, we had borrowed over $1.2 million to buy the machinery to farm the property and we still owed Wells Fargo Ag Credit more than $850,000. Without the contract, we would have to sell the equipment. And the sale price likely would not cover the loan balance. We were devastated.

After a long evening meeting with our creditors, I stood with our loan officer in the parking lot outside the King's Inn motel in Pierre. I confessed to him I was at a total loss. If the equipment sale fell short of the loan balance, we had nothing to make up the difference and the only resolution was bankruptcy. The loan officer had high regard for us and I could tell he was empathetic, but he also knew the loan had to be repaid. Failure once again. Dave and I both had families to provide for and mortgage payments to make.

When I got home, Ann was already asleep. I sat in the living room and prayed. "Dear God in Heaven, I don't know what to do. I'm scared." I ruminated for a couple of hours, then went to bed and fell into a troubled sleep. Sometime around 4:30 a.m. I awoke, alert, as if I had been awake for a long time. I thought I was hearing a voice. The message was as follows: "The owner of the property still needs farm equipment. Forget about the amount of money you have invested in the machinery. Leave the equipment to him in exchange for assuming your debt. Keep the Steiger tractor, the Chevy pickup, one Case 1370 tractor, the 12-row Allis Chalmers corn planter and the 12-row Buffalo cultivator." But I couldn't make sense of the message. The pickup was worthless, and the Steiger was the oldest tractor we owned. We had seven Case 1370 tractors, so the landowner could get by without one. But we had no land to farm. Why did we need a tractor, planter and cultivator? The exact message was repeated. There was no further explanation. I gave the voice more thought and determined it was either an answer to my prayer or just something I thought up. I settled on something I thought up and decided to discuss it with Dave the next day.

The whole concept started to make sense to us when we discussed it over coffee the next morning. We could get out of debt, which was our biggest concern. The old equipment, though of limited value, was potential equity. Maybe we *could* find land to farm.

After Dave agreed that the concept was sound, we visited our loan officer. He and the landowner agreed to the plan. Dave and I were left without debt and with some of the old farm equipment we had brought from Nebraska, plus the 1370 Case tractor. But we also were without jobs, income and land to farm. Through my anxiety, I kept hearing the words "be patient." Within two weeks, three things occurred.

First: We got an opportunity to farm. Our remaining income were fees for managing a 2,500-acre farm in northwest Nebraska, which was owned by out-of-state investors and farmed by a tenant. The tenant was moving away, and the owners needed someone to farm the land as well as manage it. That would be us!

Second: We got a call from a banker I knew in Lincoln, Nebraska, who told me he had repossessed 16,800 acres of wheat land in western South Dakota. He needed someone to farm it. That would be us!

Third: A couple of days later, a banker in a small town in eastern South Dakota called. His bank had taken over 1,500 irrigated acres in south central South Dakota. Would we be interested in farming it? Yes, that would be us! This land would be planted to corn, so we could use the twelve-row corn planter and cultivator as well as the 1370 Case tractor.

We farmed and managed all three properties for several years. We not only survived, we prospered. Within two years we were farming and/or managing more than 90,000 acres in South Dakota, Nebraska and Montana. We kept all our staff plus the office in Pierre.

In retrospect, I believe these were intercessions and the helpful guidance I received was from the same source as the *you are loved* voice. It was gentle, caring and benevolent. But I did not know the origin of the messages. They could have come from my own thoughts. They could have been manifestations of intention or answers to prayers. Perhaps these intercessions had happened frequently in my life.

If so, I had been asleep and did not recognize them.

Dave, Uncle Larry and Percy

CHAPTER 21

Back to School
1993–1995

In the months after *you are loved*, I slowly became functional at work again, and as I continued to have non-physical interactions, I began to see the intercessions were connected and they seemed to follow a progression. I was being taught lessons.

Many lessons involved books, like the one I bought that rainy night at the Barnes & Noble bookstore in Naples. I spent many hours reading, and my schooling seemed to have a pattern. As I went about my daily activities, I'd have insights which I'd ponder. Then I'd be somehow drawn to a book about it. Other times people, sometimes complete strangers, would recommend a book. Most often, I'd be directed to a book during a spontaneous visit to a bookstore, similar to having been drawn to the channeling book in Naples. Passages in the books were often relevant to what I was contemplating. They provided answers to a question, solidified an understanding or, in some cases, changed long-held beliefs.

Because of my Protestant upbringing, I believed in sin and a judgmental God. During this timeframe, I was drawn to a bookstore and I walked directly to a book entitled, *A Course in Miracles*. I was not familiar with the book and did not know that the book was a very popular channeled book about our true loving reality. I picked it up and opened it to a random page just as I had opened the Bible so many years before. One sentence of just five words stood out: "My brother, choose once again." I read it several times. The phrase was gentle but not condemning. To me it said, "You made an incorrect choice and you can make a better choice." It was loving and forgiving—qualities that were consistent with all I felt from the intercessions.

It became apparent that the voice intercessions were without ego. There was no attachment. They were just there—without judgement or expectation. This made sense to me. It was a loving presence that I felt connected to and one with—not separate or inferior.

I learned from these intercessions that I have free will and am responsible for the choices I make. My emotional reaction to a choice influences my future choices. The negative emotions surrounding the guilt and shame of my affair with a married woman, helped me avoid making that choice in the future. The new and better choice came because of the loving words—choose once again—and not from fear of punishment or damnation.

Although the lessons were progressive, there was no deadline for completing them. I felt no coercion, pressure or anxiety. I was always in control. When I completed some understanding, a loving presence led me to the next step. But it only came when I was ready.

Sometimes physical experiences related to the lessons. Like one winter day, during a 3-mile hike to a mountain I frequently visited, I began thinking my belief in the voices was absurd. A natural rock chair on top on the mountaintop was a perfect spot to sit and contemplate. I settled in, closed my eyes, and pondered the lessons I was learning. I opened my eyes and realized the short winter day had faded to darkness. For a moment I panicked, wondering how I'd find my way home. I started back down the mountain, through the forest, on a snow-covered slope. I began slipping, sliding, sometimes crashing into tree branches. As I attempted to pick myself up after the second fall, a gentle voice asked: "Do you believe the voices you hear are real?" I wanted to say, "Yes but I'm rather busy right now." But I didn't. I answered that I did believe they are real. The voice replied, "Then close your eyes, trust, listen and walk at a slow pace."

My descent was difficult with my eyes wide open. How in the world would this work? Still, I did believe so I obeyed. I closed my eyes, put my arms by my side and started to walk. My actions were not foolhardy as the slope was not steep or dangerous. Had the voice told me to jump off a cliff, I would have declined. But the voice, which was always loving, would never had done that.

I closed my eyes and began the walk taking a couple of steps down, then a step to the right or left, listening to what felt like my instinct. After a few steps, I relaxed and began to trust my intuition. I zig-zagged my way to the bottom of the slope, amazed that I never slipped or fell, didn't run into a branch or trip on an exposed rock. Not once did I open my eyes. At the bottom the voice asked, "Now do you believe in what you are experiencing?" My affirmative answer was obvious.

Another subject I contemplated was death. Do we exist beyond the death of our physical bodies? I had been asked several times by the voice, "Do you believe in death?" The related lesson began in Phoenix, Arizona, during a visit with my daughter Carly who was in school there. The night before I was scheduled to fly from Phoenix back to Pierre, I had a vivid dream. I was in a small commuter plane on a flight from Denver to Pierre seated in the front row— seat 1A. As the plane attempted to land, it crashed. I witnessed the crash, but I was no longer in my front row seat. Everyone was dead. I did not feel dead because I observed them. But I had to be dead!

I awoke in terror and jumped out of bed. I had read accounts of people who had dreams like this and did not get on a plane that subsequently crashed. To calm myself I opened the book I was reading; *A Course in Miracles*, which included a workbook with daily lessons. I opened to the lesson for the day, Lesson 14. I will never forget it. Preoccupied with my fearful thoughts, I scanned the page until I read the words "This plane crash is not real." That stopped me in my tracks.

At noon my flight from Phoenix was scheduled to leave for Denver where I would connect with the flight to Pierre. What to do? As was my habit when under stress, I walked. On the streets of Phoenix, my thoughts raced. My dream said the plane would crash. The book said it would not. I decided that, just to be safe, I'd book another flight to Pierre. As I continued walking, I thought further about a question that had recently been posed by the voice: "Do you believe in death?" Most of the time I believed we were eternal beings and survive our physical death, which is consistent with most religious thought. If I did not believe in death, it made no difference whether the plane crashed or not. Right? Well, maybe. In any case, I decided to take my scheduled flight to Denver.

Once in Denver, I walked the concourse in deep thought. The flight to Pierre was scheduled to leave in a couple of hours. I had time to ponder, worry and ruminate before I had to decide whether to get on the plane. I thought I was being taught that we survive physical death, so I finally went to the United desk to check in. The woman behind the counter handed me the boarding pass: seat 1A, the exact seat as in my terrifying dream. My stomach clenched as I walked away from the counter. Only a fool would get on that plane! I walked down the concourse at a pace that seemed to match my elevated heartrate. My mind was racing once again: "Get on the plane. No. Get on the plane. No. We die. No, we don't. Get on the plane. No."

Finally, faith in my belief we do not die prevailed. I took my place in seat 1A. Once we were airborne there was no return. With the roar of the turbo prop engines behind me, I calmed as it became clear to me that I did not believe in death. Two hours later, the pilot announced the descent into Pierre. I was in a state of total peace. I could accept either outcome, crash or not crash. I now believed we do not die.

A couple of months later, I was in Lincoln to attend the University of Nebraska football game with Pacific University. It was an afternoon game on Saturday, September 23, 1995. I was staying with Dad and Percy. Early Saturday morning the phone rang, and Percy answered. She was asked if they were the parents of Dave Snyder. Percy said yes, after which he introduced himself as Ron Anderson, the son of Harold Anderson, whom I had worked for during the summer of 1968, on their farm north of Lincoln. Ron asked how he could get in contact with me. Percy told him that I lived in South Dakota, but by coincidence, I was sitting right here. I took the phone and Ron explained that his Dad had a terminal brain tumor and was comatose most of the time, but he had asked to see me. The request seemed strange because it had been 27 years since I worked for him, and I had only seen him a couple of times since. I told Ron I was going to the football game, but I could come visit right now before the game.

As I began the 40-minute drive to their farm, the voice said to me, "You are to tell him there is no death." The message continued to repeat for the entire trip. When I arrived, Ron and his mother and sister were in the living room. I could see Harold lying on his stomach on a gurney at the far end of the dining room. His head was turned to the side and his eyes were closed. There was no movement except for labored breathing. A nurse stood near him. I visited with the family for a few minutes and then turned toward Harold. The nurse looked up and left the room. Ron had told me his Dad was no longer talking, but he might be able to hear my voice.

As I walked into the dining room, Harold did not move or open his eyes, but he said, "Dave." I walked to him, put my hand on his shoulder and delivered the message as instructed: "Harold, you need to know there is no death." As soon as I finished the sentence he exhaled. It was like air being let out of a balloon. His hand twitched and he said in an almost inaudible voice, "Thank you." I talked to him a little longer, but he made no further response. His breathing was no longer labored—it was slow and rhythmic. Ron called again the next day. His father had died peacefully that morning.

The lessons I was learning reinforced my belief that the unseen reality I was experiencing was real. It was loving and forgiving. The lessons on the mountain and in the plane, each left me with a sense of oneness with the universe and a deepening belief that our true reality extends beyond the physical world.

But it was yet another walk in the forest that would further awaken me.

CHAPTER 22

The Challenge of the Forest
1995

I have frequently hiked to the top of a mountain located about three miles east of my ranch in the Black Hills. It is higher than the surrounding mountains and is above the tree line so from the top there's a wide-open view in all four directions. One late afternoon in July 1995, I was sitting in the cabin, looking east across the meadow to a wall of trees. I was overcome with the desire to hike through the forest to the mountaintop rather than taking my customary route on the forest service trail. It was 4:00 in the afternoon but, with daylight savings time, I thought I had time to return before dark.

The wall of trees looked impenetrable which awoke in me a sense of challenge. The sun was bright, so I assumed I could maintain my sense of direction through the dense forest by following the trees' shadows. I'd have to cross rough terrain, including two ridges, but those obstacles did not deter me, they whetted my appetite for adventure. Me against the forest! Adding to the drama, I would be alone. Nobody would even know where I was—I would not even leave a note describing my route. I would succeed by myself or fail by myself. In that frame of mind, I took a long drink of water, ate an apple and set out on my quest with no provisions, dressed in shorts, a T-shirt and hiking boots.

With a sense of adventure, and a bit of trepidation, I found an opening between two large trees and entered the forest. I announced to the forest that I was there to conquer it. My announcement was a thought, but it felt like a spoken challenge. From the cabin window, the forest looked like an orderly arrangement of stately trees, but now that I was inside, it appeared formidable. Overhead, the canopy blocked the sun which I had counted on to use as a compass. A damp coolness replaced the warmth of the late summer sun. I was confronted by a maze of broken branches and deadfall. At my feet, a chaotic tangle of underbrush covered a forest floor that was matted with decaying foliage and dead wood.

I took a deep breath and considered turning back, but only briefly. I'm competitive by nature and don't quit easily, so I started walking. If the sun could not guide me, I'd rely on my intuition. I knew I had to climb two ridges and the mountain, and I laughed to myself as I realized my heart rate could be my compass. I began picking my way around bushes, branches, trees and rocks, breathing harder as I climbed. My heart beat faster, too, and soon I began to question using my intuition and my cardiac compass as guides. The undergrowth was denser than I had imagined—and, oh, those junipers. They were everywhere and blocked my path in all directions. I had no choice but to go through them and, as I proceeded, they grabbed my bare legs as if in retaliation for my intrusion. I realized I'd be scratched and bleeding by the time I reached the mountain top. The forest continued to get cooler and darker, and almost every step caused a cracking sound as dry branches broke.

When I stopped to rest, I was overcome with a sense of death and decay. Dry moss hanging on branches seemed to suck the life out of trees. Rotting pine cones and dry pine needles matted large patches of the forest floor. I imagined that if I dug underneath the dead mat I'd find a bottomless void. Frightening. The forest that had seemed like a source of life and energy when I first approached it now seemed like a tomb. The only sound was my rapidly beating heart. I tried to quiet it, afraid of being discovered, for I now felt like an invader. My loud, fast beating heart came from fear, not from exertion. I was losing my battle with the forest. My head sunk as I acknowledged my defeat and planned my retreat.

My heartbeat suddenly slowed and quieted. Then, after a long silence my rapid heartbeat returned becoming even faster and louder than before, each beat more powerful than the last. The sound seemed to be external as well as internal. It permeated the landscape, becoming deep and resonating. I sat in awe and listened. It wasn't just me, it was the heartbeat of the forest. It was joyful, vibrant, and alive, and I was part of it.

Vanished was the oppressive feeling that I was part of the death and decay around me. The environment was changing before my eyes, like a picture coming into focus. The forest now teemed with life, and I was part of it. Squirrels chirped nonstop. Birds sang in the treetops. A deer rustled the underbrush. The forest floor, which moments before had seemed like a camouflaged facade covering a bottomless abyss, now seemed to nurture new life.

I got to my feet with a new sense of energy. I was no longer the combatant. The forest was no longer the enemy. I continued my hike, but now I wasn't moving through the forest—the forest was directing me. I merged deeper and deeper into the landscape and as I did, I relinquished control and became a part of the forest. I experienced a world of harmony, balance and cooperation. An old tree on the forest floor provided a bed for seeds to grow. Rocks retarded rainfall that nurtured plants. Birds gathered branches from the forest floor to make their nests. Then, without warning my step was arrested in midair. Where my foot would have fallen was a 2-inch-tall pine tree. I sat down and laughed. Moments ago, I was thundering through the forest, a loud invader unmindful of where I stepped. No wonder I hadn't seen any wildlife.

I was no longer an intruder. I continued my trek, in the company of the forest. I didn't know where I was, but I had no sense of being lost. I was not alone but was in the company of multitudes. It was an exhilarating feeling of connection and love.

In time, I came to what looked like a solid barrier of junipers. One juniper in front of me seemed to invite me to step on it and pass through. I accepted, feeling even more in harmony with the forest. I came to a stream and as I viewed this gurgling brook, it had no beginning and no end. I was overwhelmed by a sense of eternity. There is no death—there is only life. I was part of a never-ending universe.

I left the stream and began to ascend a steep mountainside. There, through a break in the treetop canopy, I saw an outcropping of rugged, loose rock that protruded above the dense forest. It was my destination. I continued to climb, past the tree line to the summit. As I walked through the rocky area, I was embarrassed by the clattering sound I made. It was deafening compared to my quiet trek through the woods, and it reminded me of my initial, noisy intrusion into the forest.

At the top, the sun was warm, but it was beginning to set in the west. The forest below me seemed silent, and I felt alone again. Then I looked down to inspect my cut and bleeding legs. Unbelievable—there was no blood. Not even a scratch.

As I watched the daylight fade, I knew I must head home. I gazed one last time over the forested mountains. One mountain to the west had two pine trees much larger than the rest. I sensed they were looking at me. "There is a new tree on that rock outcropping," one tree seemed to say as it looked at me. "Yes, I see," the second tree said. "How long do you think he will last?" The first tree answered, "Like us, forever." They turned to me, smiled and said in unison, "Welcome."

I smiled back, bowed and said, "Thank you." A great peace came over me. Raising my tallest branches into the air, I addressed the universe:

There is no need to return home—I am home!

CHAPTER 23

Now I Am Crazy!
1995

It was dark when I returned to the cabin after my challenge of the forest hike. I got something to eat, opened my laptop and typed an account of the adventure. I wrote without pause. I felt as though I was not the one typing. The story flowed onto the page.

I had trouble going to sleep that night because my head was spinning. I had accepted some strange experiences during the past months. But, seriously, was this one real? And if it was, what did it mean?

I awoke in the middle of the night and re-read my account. It seemed preposterous. Had I dreamed it? I looked over at my dirty shorts, T-shirt and socks laying on the floor. They were proof I had indeed taken a hike, so I re-read my account a third time. In every detail it was how I remembered it. Entering the forest with bravado, seeing the death inside, experiencing the cold and the fear—I remembered it all. I also recalled the feelings of acceptance, cooperation, harmony and love. But what about being guided by the forest? Invited by junipers? Becoming one with the forest? What about the conversation with the tall pine trees? And how about waving my branches in the air? Amazing but true, I felt I had become a part of the landscape. And that I had arrived home.

During my drive to Pierre the following morning, I became concerned about my sanity. What I experienced could not have happened if I was sane. By the time I crossed the Cheyenne River, about halfway to Pierre, I was frantic. It was time to seek professional help. But what kind of help? Maybe I should start with my physician. He could refer me to a psychiatrist. But what would the psychiatrist do? Put me on drugs? Commit me? I was scared.

As I approached a small truck stop on Highway 34 called The Ridge, I felt panicky. I stopped and took a walk to clear my head. Walking around the large parking lot, a sense of calm and peace returned. I recalled the sense of cooperation I felt in the forest. There was no conflict or competition. The energy was joyful. The interactions were benevolent. I felt safe. I was safe. There was harmony. It was a place of love. None of it seemed like the experience of a person with mental illness.

I reflected on the hike in the context of my other experiences and what I had been learning. The hike seemed to reflect what I was being taught about our non-physical reality. Perhaps the hike was a real physical world experience combined with a non-physical view of what our world is supposed to be like.

After I quit combatting the forest and became a part of it, I experienced love, joy and the absence of conflict. My experience was the opposite of the hate, war, oppression and intolerance I saw on the nightly news. I had experienced a profound peace in the forest. Perhaps it was merely a representation of our non-physical reality. In theory this harmony and peace might be possible. But I shook my head in sadness as I concluded that the energy I experienced on my forest hike could not exist in our physical world. I was wrong.

I would soon discover it does exist here.

CHAPTER 24

We Are a People Company
1989–2000

A few days after my forest hike, I arrived for work one morning at D & D Farms later than usual. Laughter was coming from the break room, so I walked there rather than to my office to see what the laughter was about. The entire office staff was in the room and one of them had just told a joke. The person who told the joke retold the joke to me. I laughed, though it was one of those you-had-to-be-there moments. Regardless, I enjoyed their camaraderie. Back in my office, it hit me. The energy I discovered in the forest existed in our office and, more importantly, throughout our entire 200-employee workforce.

Our company operated in harmony. Dave and I cooperated with each other, shared in decisions and never coerced or forced decisions on each other. In 23 years in business together, we never had an argument. I had always known we had a special relationship, but now it became clear to me that our relationship provided the foundation for a company that operated in harmony and without conflict—rare but wonderful.

When we started our company in 1976, we pledged to each other to be fair and honest in our business dealings. Once, in the early, exuberant days of our partnership, we told a few friends about the pledge. One of them quipped, "That'll last about a month!" Everyone laughed in agreement. He was wrong. It lasted 23 years.

When we entered a business negotiation, we listened to what all parties wanted and arrived at a conclusion that was good for everyone. This was contrary to the zero-sum philosophy that for one to win the other must lose. To those who believe in a dog-eat-dog business world, our philosophy might sound as preposterous as my forest hike, but our experience proved it is the best way to conduct business. Negotiations were win-win transactions and our fairness and honesty were always reflected back to us. Our business dealings were without conflict and we were never sued or entangled in litigation. Did we sometimes leave money on the table? Yes. Did it compromise our success? Never.

During the expansion of our hog operation, we entered into an agreement to purchase a large parcel of land in northeast Colorado. The seller was a farmer who wanted to retire, so the deal was good for both of us. Once the purchase was finalized, I secured an option from a neighboring farmer for an additional tract of land adjacent to the farmer's property. That night I called Dave in South Dakota to review the numbers. A comparative value analysis had showed me that we had paid relatively more for the second property. I explained to Dave that, to be fair, we should pay the same for both properties. I suggested we go back to the first owner and pay him the difference, which was $20,000. Dave immediately agreed.

The next evening I sat at the kitchen table with the first farmer. I could tell he was worried that something had compromised the sale. I told him what I had discovered. "So?" he asked. I said, "To be fair, we will pay you $20,000 more at closing." He was a big man, and, despite his white hair, he was intimidating. He sat at the table in bib overalls and a blue, short-sleeved work shirt and didn't say a word. Then he leaned forward, put his massive arms on the table and said, "Are you crazy?" I replied, probably without conviction, "No." He leaned closer, looked me in the eye and said: "Sonny, when you make a deal—even if it's to your advantage—you keep it. You made your deal with me so you should keep it."

It seemed he was delivering a lesson from a wise elder to a foolish, inexperienced boy trying to become a businessman. I said, "Dave and I have discussed this and in our mind it's the right thing to do." He sat back in his chair and shrugged. We made a little small talk, probably about the weather since we were farmers and that's what farmers do. Then I drove back to town.

Later at the closing he said very little, even when his check included the additional $20,000. When we left the lawyer's office, he walked up to me on the sidewalk and shook my hand. "Dave, my wife and I talked about our conversation. You were right. We wish the two of you the best of luck. Thank you for buying our land." I noticed he had called me Dave, not Sonny. His comments reminded me that the positive energy I had observed in the forest was reflective—that is, when you send out joy, benevolence and harmony, they were returned in kind.

As I became more aware of the similarities between the loving forest and D & D Farms, my management style changed. I had been programmed to follow the male-dominated, top-down style of management. Now I discovered I was becoming an observer, watching how our staff worked in cooperation with each other. I became less involved in the daily activities of the company, trusting and supporting the decisions made by our employees, even when the decision had a negative impact on the company.

Dave and I did not criticize our employees when they made mistakes and, as a result, they didn't fear being chastised, berated, lectured, ridiculed or fired. They felt safe and supported because they were. They felt empowered to take responsibility and knew we would support them in their efforts to correct any mistake. In other words, because they felt safe, they were able to perform at their highest level, which was to the maximum benefit to the company.

Our employees exemplified a loving, caring and happy family. There were no conflicts or inequalities regardless of race, sex or position in the company. If someone had to miss work, others picked up the slack. On their own, our employees created a policy to pool their unused sick leave for employees who had exhausted their own.

Care and concern for the animals we raised was also a manifestation of the loving energy at D & D Farms. When I walked through our farrowing rooms where the sows gave birth, staff working there often picked up a baby pig and, with pride, gave it to me to hold. They cared for the mother sows and newborn piglets in a quiet, caring and loving manner. Farrowing rooms, where piglets were born, were ventilated and warmed to provide a constant temperature environment. Because of the design of the buildings, piglets were protected from being accidently squashed by their mothers, a common hazard on traditional farms. Our growing animals had room to move around from feeding areas to sleeping areas. They were safe from outside weather extremes.

We hired Temple Grandin, world-renowned expert in animal behavior from Colorado State University, to teach us even more ways to interact with animals in a kind manner, right down to the color of clothes we should wear for different tasks. Our movements were quiet and gentle when we moved through the hog buildings, which was calming to the animals. To my surprise, the calm animals resulted in a calm workforce. Raising pigs this way, protected from the elements, was more humane to me than the way we raised them when I was growing up. That said, Dad was gentle when caring for livestock, and he had taught me that we were their caretakers. On that cold Christmas Eve in the barn with the sheep as a young teenager, I had learned firsthand that animals are intuitive and sense a connection to us. In the same way I had felt connected to the sheep on the Christmas Eve in the barn, my hike in the forest strengthened my sense of connection with all life on earth.

Although I was president and CEO of D & D Farms, I didn't fully appreciate the loving and cooperative culture of our company. One day Gloria Hanson, our human resources director, told me that some staff, including upper management, wanted a company motto. A couple of thoughts popped out of my mouth, along the lines of "We work in hog heaven." Gloria laughed but assured me the staff was serious.

Several weeks later Gloria came into my office. "Well, the motto is done and agreed to by everyone including Dave. What do you think it is?" She was smiling, so I said, I'll bet it's 'Pigs R Us.' She laughed as she handed me a piece of paper and said, "Not even close." I took it and read the new company motto:

"We are a people company, we just happen to raise hogs."

I was speechless. I leaned back in my chair and let the meaning of the words sink in. It was a Friday afternoon and late that day I headed for the ranch in the Black Hills. As I drove across the open prairie of western South Dakota, I continued to think about the new motto. I was beginning to understand how much I learned from being the president of a company with such wonderful employees. The lessons went far beyond the subject of hog production. We were a family. My partner, Dave, was more like a brother than a business associate. I felt fortunate and grateful.

Most importantly, the primary lesson I learned from our motto was that the loving, cooperative energy I experienced during my hike in the forest was playing out before my very eyes, in our own company, in the physical world.

Perhaps it must happen everywhere, if our human species is to survive.

Dave Luers—business partner and pilot of the Cessna 340A company plane

Dave Snyder and D & D Farms management staff

CHAPTER 25

The End of D & D Farms
2000

W e completed the planned growth and expansion of D & D Farms in 1997. We now employed almost 200 employees with annual production approaching 400,000 market hogs. Every weekday seven semi-loads totaling more than 1500 hogs left for market. Our company capitalization was $65 million, and with annual sales of approximately $40 million, we were now one of the 25 largest pork producers in the country.

To ensure we weren't undercapitalized in a risky business, Dave and I raised outside capital by selling investment interests to accredited investors in a series of limited partnerships. D & D Farms was the general partner in each of the partnerships. This reduced our financial risk but also reduced our percentage of ownership. At the beginning of 1997, we had five of these partnerships and a total of 65 investors, many of whom lived in Arizona. Hormel Foods was the largest investor, and they held a contract for the marketed hogs. Many of the investors, including Hormel, were investors in more than one partnership.

By late 1997, we had completed our growth. In early 1998, I had a very strong and persistent feeling that we should combine the partnerships into one corporate entity. We were fortunate to have an experienced board of directors, which included: an investment banker, the CEO of a large publicly traded company, the president of a national bank, a prominent lawyer and an accomplished accountant, as well as the executive vice president of Hormel Foods. Dave and I valued their advice and wisdom. When I raised the consolidation idea at a board meeting, the directors' collective opinion was that it would be impossible. They believed we would not be able to find a fair way to combine the different entities. The partnerships had been created at different times. Tax liabilities, equity values, different rates of earning and varying stages of depreciation would make consolidation impossibly complicated. Besides, the partnerships were working well and were profitable. Don't fix something that isn't broken. So, I dropped the idea.

However, I left the meeting still convinced we needed to consolidate the partnerships. I became almost obsessed with the idea—driven by something I could not identify. I'm competitive, and I might have felt challenged because no one else thought I could do it. But that didn't feel like the source of my obsession, nor was there any compelling business reason. Despite this, I went to work creating spreadsheet after spreadsheet, trying to figure out a solution. Spreadsheet analysis was my strong suit, so I thought there must be a mathematical way to accomplish the consolidation. After many nights and weekends at the computer, I began to see a possible way through the tangle of partnerships. The accountant on our board was a brilliant resource, and I began communicating with him by phone and email. His analysis helped me move forward, and a path to consolidation began to emerge, even though he did not understand why I was spending so much energy on it.

Then I saw it. Not only could we consolidate, but afterwards, all the partners would be in a better financial position—unless we sold the company in the next five years, which we had no plans of doing. Once I finished the how, and I confirmed the math with our accountant director, I again presented the consolidation plan to the board. This time, after hearing my mathematical solution with the support from the accountant, the board unanimously approved the plan. Our stockholders subsequently approved the plan, and by early spring 1998, we became one happy consolidated corporate family.

The consolidation was an almost miraculous solution to a near impossible challenge, but I kept asking myself what was behind my compulsion to create it? There were business advantages, but they weren't necessary or compelling. It was a mystery.

Several months later an unfortunate circumstance caused the mystery to be solved. An unprecedented expansion of the hog industry caused supply to far exceed demand. The bottom fell out of the market. By the fall of 1998, hog prices fell to a low of around 8 cents per pound, but production costs remained at about 45 cents per pound. Everyone in the industry, including D & D Farms, was financially devastated. Many of our competitors filed bankruptcy or were purchased in a massive industry consolidation. By early 1999, when prices began to recover, we had lost most of our equity. Fortunately, we began with high levels of equity before the price collapse. But had we not consolidated, a couple of our partnerships would have faced bankruptcy.

Maybe my obsession to consolidate was luck. Maybe it was intuition, or just good business sense. It's true that, once consolidated, we could borrow money at a lower rate, and the combined companies were easier to manage. But those factors were not what had driven me with such compulsion. Nor did I, or anyone else in the industry, foresee the collapse of hog prices.

I recognized that it was not the first time I received help from an inexplicable source when I needed it most. I believe my compulsion came from that part of reality that sees more than I can see in the physical world.

Although we remained in compliance with our loan covenants, Dave and I foresaw a long road ahead—perhaps 10 years—to recover our lost equity, let alone earn returns for our stockholders.

We decided the best business decision was to sell the company. It wasn't a light decision—our livelihood and the livelihoods of our employees depended on D & D Farms.

Once the decision was made, Dave insisted our price had to be at or near our capitalized value of $65 million, which would return the money we lost. I pointed out to him that our current market value was $35 to $45 million, but he held firm to his position. I was resolved to return our stockholder's initial investment, which would require, coincidentally, a selling price of about $65 million. We went to the board in agreement, telling them we should sell the company if we could get $65M. The directors knew the market and some wondered what Dave and I were smoking. Even though they agreed with us that the sale would be our best strategy, they told us it would be impossible to find a buyer at that high a price. After much discussion we convinced them it wouldn't hurt to try.

Soon after, Dave got a call from Seaboard Corporation asking if we would consider selling. He gave them our price, and they came back with an offer of $62 million. We accepted their offer and I signed an agreement to purchase on December 7, 1999, at our corporate attorney's office in Phoenix. After several months of due diligence, we closed the sale on March 31, 2000. When all the assets were valued, as per Dave and my intentions, the final sale price was $65 million. Comparable sales of companies around that time revealed that our sale price was a huge positive anomaly. How did this happen? Right place at the right time? No matter what the cause or chain of events, our intentions had manifested into reality.

End of story? Not quite. While the sale returned the initial investment to our investors, Dave and I, as original investors, would get hammered by ordinary income tax recapture. We'd walk away with very little money. A tragic ending to our 23 years of business together. We had understood this would happen when we decided to sell, but we knew the sale was best for the stockholders.

The night before I was to sign the purchase agreement in Phoenix on December 7th, I called Dave in South Dakota and asked if
he was sure I should go ahead and sign? He said yes, it was the
right thing to do for our stockholders. I agreed. I hung up the
phone and sat silently in my hotel room. I felt the agony of one
more financial disaster. It had been a long day. I went into the
bathroom to rinse my face. When I looked in the mirror, I again
saw myself as the old man walking the street in Pierre as I had so
many years before. Perhaps too old to start over. I went to bed to
try and get some much-needed sleep before our contract signing in
the morning.

At about 4 a.m. a familiar voice awakened me with instructions
to go to my computer. As in the past, I was completely awake in an
instant and I obeyed. I was then instructed to type the following:
"Seller may allocate good will among its stockholders in any manner it chooses, so long as there are no adverse tax consequences to
buyer." I was further instructed that the purchase agreement needed to include this clause. I didn't understand what it meant and why
it should be included in the contract. I returned to bed and went
back to sleep.

About an hour later I awoke with a start. I thought I might understand the reason for the clause. I got up and turned on my laptop and opened my much-used Consolidate D & D Farms
Worksheet. I made a few formula changes and started to play
around with the good will. According to my new calculations, if we
could re-allocate the value of the good will and the IRS approved,
Dave and I could solve our net-cash inequality problem without
negatively affecting our other stockholders or Seaboard. Amazing!

Before the contract signing meeting began, I presented a copy
of what I had typed to our one director who was there for the
meeting. I told him we needed to have Seaboard agree to include it
in the contract. He read it and asked, "What the hell does this
mean, Dave?" I told him I wasn't a tax expert, but I thought it

might solve the income tax recapture problem. I pointed out that, since the wording in the clause allowing for the re-allocation was at our option, we could put the clause in the contract, then check later with the IRS to see if it was legal. If it was legal, we could re-allocate the good will but only if it was to our benefit. When the meeting began, the president of Seaboard read the new clause and handed it to their attorney. They excused themselves. My heart was racing. When they returned the president said, "We don't have a problem with including the clause." Everyone signed.

Immediately after the signing, my director called a nationally re-nowned tax expert whom he knew. His office was a few miles away and to our surprise he was available. Within a half an hour we were in his office presenting the clause and my calculations to him. He said he'd get right to work on it. Later that afternoon he called to inform us that, since the net taxes paid were the same regardless of the way the good will was allocated, the IRS would not have a problem with the clause. My calculations were correct, the advice given was correct and we all came out financially whole following the sale. Even Dave and me.

Most of the intercessions I had previously experienced were re-sponses to my requests. This was not the case in the middle-of-night intercession that solved the tax inequality problem related to the sale of our company. Dave and I had accepted the terms of the contract before I went to bed. I had not asked for a solution—no request, no thought, no wish, no prayer. The intercession came to our benefit without request and in a manner where everyone was a winner. My perception of the intercessions from our non-physical world was expanded.

Is this presence always with us or are we part of it?

CHAPTER 26

The Journey Continues
2001

With the sale of D & D Farms, my life changed. I was retired, so I sold the house on the Missouri River in Pierre and moved to the ranch in the Black Hills, a long-held dream come true. I spent the next three years converting the combination cabin-garage into a real house. I constructed another building to be used as a shop and to store machinery. I built new fences and a dam to create a pond. After being in management for years, I was back on the land driving tractors, backhoes, bulldozers and skid steers. I spent many hours operating a chain saw. I relished the physical work and the long hours on the machines.

Dave with Uncle Larry, cousins Darryl Frerichs and Will Rennick when visiting the ranch

I continued to experience events I could not explain. Some were small, others more significant. I now knew without a doubt, they were real, even if science couldn't explain them. The experiences I was having were of two distinct types.

One type was related to my focused intention, which created manifestations in the future. An interesting feature was their lack of linearity in time. Events necessary to create future manifestations often happened before I had the intention. The process seemed to operate beyond time and didn't follow the laws of cause and effect.

Others were intercessions which were helpful and benevolent. Often, they were unconnected to my thoughts or requests, such as the contract clause in the D & D Farms sale.

I was a member of a volunteer committee responsible for the annual Mickelson Trail Bicycle Trek held in the Black Hills in September of each year. In 2001, the 109-mile bicycle ride was scheduled for the weekend of September 14-16. On the Tuesday morning before the ride—the September 11th no one will ever forget—I watched the towers of the World Trade Center collapse. Like everyone, I was overwhelmed with shock and horror. On Friday, just three days away, our trail trek would begin. Do we cancel it? I called my co-chair and, after sharing our grief and discussing options, we called a committee meeting. The committee decided to hold the ride as scheduled because many riders were already on the road, driving to the Black Hills.

I was responsible for the welcoming remarks before the ride. I tried to write the speech, but words would not come. By midnight on Wednesday, I had written nothing. I was in a panic. I went to bed, but just rolled around trying to decide what to say. I fell asleep from sheer exhaustion.

I awoke at 4:30 a.m., alert to the voice giving instructions to go to my computer. I typed without deliberating or pausing. Then I read what I had typed. Thank you, I thought. Thank you. I went back to bed and fell into a peaceful sleep.

I awoke late, put on the coffee and printed what I had written. I sat in my customary chair, absorbing the heat from the coffee cup I held in my hand.

Slowly I read the words I had typed:

Historically, the Lakota have always acknowledged the spiritual nature of the Black Hills. Although in perhaps not the same way, many of us who now live in these Hills also experience this spirituality. For those of you who have come here for the first time, you are about to experience a very special place.

This is a place of healing and it is my hope that as this tragic week comes to an end, those of us here can let the landscape and the forest help with our individual healing.

Let the ride today to Edgemont, with its sweeping vistas, enable us to see beyond this week. Let the breeze in our faces dry our tears. Let the flowers still surviving, now almost out of season, remind us of our human tenacity and resolve.

Let the streams we pass give us solace in their rhythmic undulations and let these streams, that seem as we view them to have no beginning and no end, give us comfort that all life extends beyond any one moment in time.

Let us remember, as we view the beautiful fall colors in the grasses and the trees, that everything has its season and all that has come before will pass away and come once again. Let the majesty of the trees envelop us with their strength as we ride through their midst. Let the ancient rock formations we pass remind us of our strength and our eternity.

Let the joy, the laughter, the camaraderie and the community we enjoy this weekend, remind us we are loving beings, and without love we would feel no pain, no anguish, no grief for the events of this past week.

One of the original posters made for the Mickelson Trail is an appropriate mantra for this weekend. In the poster, the trail speaks to all of us. The caption reads, "Come to me, I will awaken your spirit and restore your soul." May this be a joyous and healing weekend for all.

After re-reading what I had typed, I looked out the window of my home, gazing at the sacred land of the Black Hills. I gave thanks for the words. They were not mine. I was the typist. On Friday morning when I addressed the crowd of bicyclists, they stood in silence as I read the words that had been given to me. Occasionally I had to pause as emotions welled up within me—not just the emotion of grief but also the emotion of gratitude for the source of the words. I was grateful for the spiritual intercession. It was a healing weekend for all.

Often my experiences were less consequential and they affected only me.

In March 2004, during a trip to Disney World with my oldest daughter's family, I told them I was thinking about taking a trip to the Caribbean. On the flight home I pondered who I could ask to accompany me. When I arrived home a couple of days later, I had a message from a friend, Meredith, who lived in Virginia. I returned her call and she told me she had won a time-share vacation in Aruba at a silent auction. Would I like to accompany her? My focus on a Caribbean vacation had manifested into physical reality.

I booked a flight through Dulles airport in Washington D.C. and emailed my flight information to Meredith. She replied to my email to inform me that she had already booked her own ticket for the same flight. She was assigned seat 8A and asked me to try and get the seat next to her. My seat had already been assigned but I didn't know what it was. When I received my ticket, I was amazed to see I had been assigned seat 8C. The flight was full except for one seat. 8B was empty.

I recognized there was a non-linearity of events from thought to manifestation. Meredith had the time-share vacation before I thought about a trip to the Caribbean. My seat was assigned before she asked me to sit beside her. And the only empty seat on the plane was 8B. Was this all coincidental? There was much I did not comprehend about this new reality I was experiencing.

Often the intercessions were repeated, like the sequence of waking at the exact time on the clock. These repetitions gave me comfort that something larger than me was involved in my life.

In August 2004, South Dakota Governor Mike Rounds asked me to serve on the first board of directors for the new South Dakota Science and Technology Authority. I paused for a moment and then asked, "Is this a joke?" I reminded him I had farmed all my life and my degrees were in Agricultural Economics. He laughed but assured me it was not a joke. He wanted some board members who had a business background.

The Governor was leading an effort to convert the recently closed 8,000-foot-deep Homestake Gold Mine in Lead, South Dakota, into a national underground science laboratory. There, physicists would conduct experiments to try and discover dark matter and research subatomic particles like neutrinos. Deep underground labs protect sensitive experiments from the interference of cosmic radiation, and this potential lab would be the largest, deepest lab of this type in the world. On the economic side, the lab could provide significant benefits to South Dakota, and the town of Lead, just 11 miles from my ranch.

Homestake was one of eight sites around the country being proposed for the underground lab. A competition was under way, and the National Science Foundation was the judge. We needed a strategy to win that competition. The Governor explained the biggest challenge was acquiring the closed mine. Homestake was owned by Barrick Gold Corp., an international mining company based in Toronto, Canada and he wanted them to donate the closed mine to the State of South Dakota. In principle, Barrick officials didn't oppose donating the mine for science, but they were unwilling to expose their company to potential liability for an underground laboratory.

I accepted the governor's offer. After I hung up I thought back to a 2001 newspaper article I had read about the potential laboratory. After reading the article I had a persistent thought that I would be involved, but I dismissed it as preposterous and perhaps even arrogant. I was a retired farmer with no science background. Now, three years later, I was an active participant.

The first board meeting was held in August 2004. To my surprise, I was elected chairman. Soon after, the executive director of the Science Authority resigned, and my fellow board members asked me to become the executive director—an even greater surprise. I hesitated, but agreed to serve for six months, until the board could find a permanent director—or more accurately, a real director.

When I walked into my predecessor's office on my first day as Executive Director, it was cleared of his possessions. I had the empty feeling that the knowledge that was necessary for my new responsibilities had walked out the door with him. My appointment must be a huge mistake—perhaps a cosmic mistake! I almost laughed. Crying would have been more appropriate.

I left the office and headed outside for a much-needed walk. Please give me a sign I am supposed to be here. It was a thought as much as a prayer or request. The next day a friend congratulated me on my appointment and said, "You're the perfect person to make this happen." A little later a female acquaintance said, "If anyone can make this happen, you can." Their confidence didn't reassure me. But within the next few days other people came up to me and repeated the same words—exactly. When the encounters ended, each of the two comments had been repeated four times. Although I did not know the why of my appointment, the repetitions assured me I was supposed to be the executive director. I served in the position not for six months, but for almost four years.

We were successful in convincing Barrick Gold to donate the mine property and South Dakota was selected as the site for the potential underground lab. The Sanford Underground Research

Facility now conducts scientific research a mile deep in the abandoned Homestake gold mine.

As it turned out, I did play a role. My business background enabled me to understand Barrick's issues in donating the property and come up with solutions. My experience with contract negotiations was instrumental in the seven-month process of creating the Property Donation Agreement with multiple attorneys on both sides. My experience in budgeting and cash flow development helped create the fiscal numbers necessary to obtain a $19.9M appropriation at a special session of the South Dakota legislature.

However, without the repeated intercessions, I would never have had the confidence needed to fulfill the responsibilities of my position. I retired in June 2008 and returned to life on the ranch.

I was close to the final step to creating a spiritual sanctuary.

Dave Snyder to resign from science authority

LABORATORY-PROJECT SHEPHERD TO REMAIN AVAILABLE AS A
CONSULTANT

Dave Snyder, who was a key player in transforming the shuttered Homestake gold mine to being named the National Science Foundation's choice for a national deep underground science lab, announced Friday that he is resigning as executive director of the South Dakota Science and Technology Authority. (Journal file photo)

November 15, 2007 11:00 pm • Bill Harlan, Journal staff

Rapid City Journal newspaper article

CHAPTER 27

The Last Dot
2009

As I once again settled into my retirement, I spent several months traveling and making further improvements to the ranch. Over the years, it had become increasingly sacred to me. I was its caretaker and protector, and I understood the ranch was not for my benefit alone. It was to be shared. It had a purpose beyond my use and enjoyment.

Now in 2009, I began to contemplate the bigger picture for the ranch. Something was to be created here. But what? The answer came in unexpected detail.

I had purchased a large piece of abstract art from an artist in Indianapolis, Indiana. I decided to drive to Indianapolis in my pickup to get it. I always enjoyed road trips because, just like driving a tractor, they provided good thinking time. As an added benefit, I could return home through Kansas City and visit my daughters and their families. I made the trip in early spring and looked forward to driving time allowing for reflection about what the ranch was to become.

While driving on a stretch of Interstate 70 through Illinois on the way from Indianapolis to Kansas City, the gentle voice returned and said, "Drive to the side of the highway, stop and put on your flashers. Write this down." I was not near an exit and the mention of flashers seemed to mean I was to pull off the highway now. I pulled over, put on my flashers, and got a tablet and pencil out of my briefcase. I was ready to write.

"The name will be Pathways Spiritual Sanctuary." After a pause the voice continued, explaining that the entrance to the sanctuary would be a solid wooden gate within a solid wooden fence, which would visually and physically separate a parking area for visitors from the sanctuary. The solid gate would serve as a portal into a sacred space. As I wrote the words onto my tablet, I could visualize the entrance.

The voice continued, "There will be an entry prayer of affirmation on a bronze plaque for people to read when they enter the sanctuary. Write this down."

Entry Prayer of Affirmation

I enter this sacred space with gratitude. I walk these pathways with love, compassion, tolerance and forgiveness for myself and all others.

I honor those who have walked this land before my time. I ask they join me in Spirit and embrace and guide me while in this Spiritual Sanctuary.

The voice continued: "There will also be an exit prayer of affirmation on a similar bronze plaque for people to read when they exit. Write this down."

Exit Prayer of Affirmation

I leave this sacred space committed to continue walking a path of love, compassion, tolerance and forgiveness, for myself and all others.

I leave with gratitude and a lightened heart.

The voice then described how the bronze plaques would be attached to concrete bases placed on pedestals. In the concrete on each base there would be recessed handprints of a man, woman and child for the purpose of enabling visitors to place their hands in the recessed handprints while reading the words. This would connect them to the sacred land.

I read my handwritten words several times. The name for the sanctuary and all other instructions seemed right. As I returned to the road, I could envision the gate and knew where it would be located. I could imagine the plaques and handprints in the concrete.

The voice continued as I drove. "There will be a walking path, circular in nature, which will lead back to the gate, allowing the same gate to be used for both the entrance and exit." Additional details were revealed as I continued my drive to Kansas City.

Although I liked the name, it didn't sound unique and I began to doubt it would be available as either a domain name or non-profit corporation name, so I tried not to get too attached to it. But I should not have worried. An internet search disclosed Pathways Spiritual Sanctuary domain and corporate names were available. I wasted no time in registering the name and by fall 2009, creation of Pathways Spiritual Sanctuary had begun.

The words, *love, compassion, tolerance and forgiveness for myself and all others* were on both the entry and exit plaques. The words resonated with my experience in the forest, and they described the energy Dave and I, and our employees, enjoyed during the years of D & D Farms.

The phrase, *for myself and all others* struck a spot deep within me as I remembered the intercession *you are loved.* Looking back on the long journey through my life, I now felt loved. As I acknowledged the difficulty of maneuvering through all the twists and turns of my life, I felt compassion for myself. I felt tolerance for my mistakes and I released judgement of all the wrongs I had done. I felt forgiven.

Words on the entry plaque also invited those who walked this land before me to join me, embrace me and guide me while in the sanctuary. This phrase tied the visiting experience to the loving energy of the spiritual realm I continued to experience at the ranch. Yes, the plaques were correct, and I envisioned visitors placing their hands in the molds connecting them to the spirit and sacredness of the beautiful land.

While on a driving trip to Phoenix fifteen years earlier, I stopped in Santa Fe, New Mexico where I visited the city square. I saw a monumental bronze statue located outside one of the galleries. The sculpture was about fourteen feet tall and it was a life-sized image of a Plains Indian astride a horse, holding a buffalo skull to the heavens. It was titled *The Invocation*. It was the most powerful bronze I had ever seen, and I sat there viewing it for over an hour.

At the time I did not know what my plans were for the ranch, but I knew this statue would be an important part of whatever was to be created. It honored the Lakota and the sacredness of the Black Hills.

Now in 2009 I was ready to begin work on creating a spiritual sanctuary at the ranch. I contacted the artist, Buck McCain, who lived in Tucson, Arizona, and asked if he could make *The Invocation* for me. He said the rubber molds had not been used for over a decade and he doubted they would be good enough to make another statue. He didn't know if they even still existed. If they did, they would be stored somewhere at Shidoni Foundry in Santa Fe where the statue had been made. He offered to drive to Santa Fe to look for them. He found the molds and all but one was good enough for one more pour.

In 2004, I had requested I be taken out of Dad and Percy's will because I felt I did not need the money from their estate. They were reluctant but they honored my request. But, shortly before Percy died in 2007, they informed me I had been put back in the will. Dad explained I had always been benevolent with my money and they preferred I receive my share. I could use it for a charitable purpose.

In September of 2009, I made a trip to Lincoln specifically to have a conversation with Dad. We sat in the living room while I explained the concept for Pathways Spiritual Sanctuary. I described *The Invocation* bronze statue, how I had seen it years ago in Santa Fe and now felt it needed to be part of the sanctuary. I told him the cost. As I presumed, he could not comprehend spending that much money on a bronze statue. Nevertheless, I asked Dad if he would approve dedicating my future inheritance to the cost of the statue. He didn't hesitate—he replied he was inspired and moved with the concept of Pathways Spiritual Sanctuary. He was pleased that his estate could play a role in its creation. The last defective mold was remade, and *The Invocation* now greets visitors as they begin their visit at Pathways Spiritual Sanctuary.

Dad's knowledge of my intent to use my inheritance for the purchase of the statue connected him with the sanctuary. Because my inheritance would not be available until after Dad's death, I used my own money to purchase *The Invocation*. Once the statue was in place, I sometimes began our telephone visits by jokingly asking him, "How are you feeling, Dad?" He would laugh and reply, "Sorry Dave, I feel pretty good. I think I'll be around a while longer." Our wounded relationship was healing.

Over the next few months and into 2010, more details of what would be in the sanctuary continued to come to me. A large labyrinth was constructed in a clearing in the aspen grove. Bronze plaques were located along the pathways with quotes from contemporary, religious and historical figures. A bronze statue of a seated angel with a small boy on her lap was placed within a grove of aspen trees as a tribute to my mother.

When Pathways Spiritual Sanctuary was completed in July 2010, I walked the pathway one last time before opening the gate to the public. *The Invocation* greeted me as I entered. I walked with a sense of fulfillment and a connection to this sacred land. I had awakened to a remarkable spiritual world, and I felt grateful to the inner voice that guided me in the creation of the sanctuary. It had been a long journey from the Turkey Shack to pig farming to Pathways.

The last dot was connected.

CHAPTER 28

The Gate is Open
2010

The gate to Pathways Spiritual Sanctuary opened to the public on July 17, 2010. On July 18, the day after the opening and dedication ceremony, I walked the path in solitude. There were no visitors, and none the next day, nor the next. I began to question myself. What had I done? The sanctuary had been a project like building the baseball field in the movie *Field of Dreams*. Build it and they will come. But no one came. Several days later I was relieved to see one car in the parking lot. Over the next few weeks, the number of cars in the lot increased.

Each year since 2010, Pathways has been open from mid-May until the end of October. Since the opening, thousands of visitors have walked through the gate. There is no charge to those who visit. Pathways is a place where all are welcome regardless of who they are or what they believe. It has no connection to any one belief or theology. Pathways is not advertised. Those who visit for the first time have usually heard about it from other people.

Inside the gate, visitors are invited to place their hands on the hand imprints in the concrete while reading the Entry Prayer of Affirmation. As they begin walking the path, they come to the first of several bronze plaques along the 1½-mile path. The words on the first plaque were written by American author and poet Jane Yolen.

HUSH,
THIS IS A HOLY PLACE,
A SACRED PLACE,
WHERE THE VISIONS DWELL,
WHERE THE DREAMING
OF A RACE BEGAN.
SOMEONE'S GOD
HAS STEPPED HERE,
SLEPT HERE,
KNELT HERE,
DWELT HERE,
SPOKEN HERE OF LIFE,
OF DEATH,
OF HOLY THINGS.
WHEN YOU COME,
COME SOFTLY,
WALK SOFTLY,
TALK SOFTLY,
BE MINDFUL OF THE DREAMS.
THIS IS A SACRED PLACE.
HUSH.

After the Jane Yolen plaque, visitors walk around a bend on the path where *The Invocation* is framed by an expansive view of the mountain meadow. The 14-foot monumental bronze depicting a Native American sitting astride his horse with arms reaching to the heavens, invokes a sense of spirituality.

A visitor from France wrote an emotional story about her experience at Pathways Spiritual Sanctuary which was published in the November 2013 issue of the French magazine HOZHO. She described how, at *The Invocation* bronze statue, the rider appeared to dismount and walked with her on the path. She describes their conversation as they walked. Her story reminded me of my own experience while building the gate. As I worked, I felt Native

American elders around me. They were jubilant, and they offered to serve as greeters and accompany visitors on their walk.

After *The Invocation*, visitors walk through an aspen forest, where they find another plaque.

WHY PATHWAYS SPIRITUAL SANCTUARY?

We live in a time that often seems dominated by separateness, a separateness that results in human conflict and contentious interactions. This is true of interactions on an individual level as well as those on a collective scale, where they have societal, political and international implications. This separateness also results in conflict with our environment and other life on our planet.

At the same time, regardless of our personal realities or experiences, there is a place deep within us where we recognize that all life is connected. From this perspective, we can view our outer world with love, compassion, tolerance and forgiveness.

WHAT IS PATHWAYS SPIRITUAL SANCTUARY?

Pathways is a quiet place to spend time walking, sitting, contemplating, reflecting or healing in the natural landscape of the sacred Black Hills. The theme of Pathways Spiritual Sanctuary is "Beyond Belief," for Pathways stands beyond the diversity of beliefs, race, religions, cultures, personal histories and life experiences. Pathways is preserved for all who choose to come. Within the Sanctuary, all can walk as one and honor the sacredness of all life and Mother Earth.

Within the sanctuary there is an intimate connection with our Mother Earth. The following three plaques located along the pathway exemplify this connection and the same sense of oneness that I discovered on my challenge of the forest walk.

This we know . . . The earth does not belong to man; man belongs to the earth. Whatever befalls the earth befalls the sons of the earth. All things are connected like the blood that unites a family. Man did not weave the web of life; he is merely a strand in it. Whatever he does to the web he does to himself. —Chief Seattle, 1854 (Attributed)

Underneath the surface appearance, everything is not only connected with everything else, but also with the Source of all life out of which it came. Even a stone, and more easily a flower or a bird, could show you the way back to God, to the source, to yourself. When you look at it or hold it and let it be without imposing a word or mental label on it, a sense of awe, of wonder, arises within you and reflects your own essence back to you. —Eckhart Tolle

A human being is a part of the whole called by us Universe, a part limited in time and space. He experiences himself, his thoughts and feelings as something separated from the rest, a kind of delusion of his consciousness. This delusion is a kind of prison for us, restricting us to our personal desires and to affection for a few persons nearest to us. Our task must be to free ourselves from this prison by widening our circle of compassion to embrace all living creatures and the whole of nature in its beauty. —Albert Einstein

Journal entries written by visitors often demonstrate that they feel connected, not separate during their time at Pathways.

"I thought when I came here I would just sit and read— but now I find I come here just to be—be in the present, the now—in the sounds of the birds, in the sound of the wind in the trees—in the quiet—away from all the hustle and bustle —Just to be." —Char R.

"This is what life is about: nature, flowers, trees, springs, ponds, breeze, sky, birds, moles, butterflies, calming, and becoming one with nature. For this I am grateful." —Lori R.

"I honor that place in you in which the whole universe dwells. I honor that place in you which is of light, truth, peace, love and all that is holy —when you are in that place in me—we are one—we are unity."—quote from Ram Das

"Peace, joy, love, forgiveness, patience, gratitude—give these to others and you give them to yourself—Beyond Gorgeous! Gracias! My mother, nearly 80, and I walked, smelled, saw and felt the love here. Bless you for your thoughtful sharing. May the entire world know the peace that is here."—no name

"As I travel this path, I become more in tune with nature. I take this moment to reflect upon my life."—no name

"I have had many travels around the world, but never have I seen a place so full of such natural beauty."—no name.

"This is such a sacred place and the gentle breeze, warm sunshine and babbling brook soothed my soul and I once again remember and feel my connectedness to ALL!"—no name

I came across a man sitting cross-legged near *The Invocation*. He appeared to be in his 50s. He wore jeans and a shirt with sleeves cut off. His hair was in a ponytail and his full beard extended to his chest. His arms were covered with tattoos and he would have looked more natural at the Sturgis Motorcycle Rally than in a spiritual sanctuary. He looked up at me and said, "I have lived in this area all my life and have been in every part of the Blacks Hills. I don't know what it is here, but it is different. I come here and just weep."

This unique energy is often reflected in journal entries. The following was written at the sanctuary's Twisted Root Bench by an unknown visitor.

"I am a skeptic to the core. If I can't see it or touch it, it does not exist. But there is something in this place I cannot explain. I feel joy, sorrow, peace, beauty and a whole range of human emotions, all at the same time. Some may say it is God, others may say it is a natural energy. I'm okay with not knowing. All I do know is that I feel home here, and I hope you do as well."

Once, when I walked through the gate, a woman stood at the entry plaque with her hands in the indented handprints. She was sobbing so I attempted to back out without disturbing her. But she heard me and walked over and asked me to hold her. I agreed and held her as she cried. When her crying subsided, she explained her tears: "I was always told to be loving, compassionate, tolerant and forgiving for others." Her tears returned. "But never ever for myself." She seemed to be releasing a lifetime of hidden pain and guilt. As I reflected on my life journey I could understand her tears. I marveled at the wisdom and value of the guidance that had been given to me in creating Pathways.

Many journal entries describe Pathways as a place of healing.

"What an inspiring journey this is. We have cleansed, re-focused, re-energized and have been truly lifted to a higher level of life. God is amazing for bringing us the messengers and the facilities to truly love one another. This is a day of transformation."—Jody K.

"There is healing energy here."—Pam from Denver

"I had a wonderful vision of my life ahead —the direction I was looking for. I also felt the release of what was holding me back..."—ND

"The tears, they flow and what a release—how much I need to heal. The sculpture of the angel—The Divine Mother in my eyes—and the child of perfect peaceful innocence. ... Love—realizing that it must come from within first."—Tracy

"I thirst for solitude. I thirst for calm, for the gifts that come from the silence and the sunshine trickling through the leaves of the aspen on a day of gratitude and forgiveness. — Namaste — "Lost sister friend"

"You will be missed, and you will be loved until we meet again."—no name

"So emotional—Sad—What have I missed? What are we doing? 78 years of age."—no name

"I lost my mom a year ago today. Thinking of her in this beautiful place with tears and good memories."—no name

"Today is the day! For me to put my thoughts out. I have been here a half dozen times or more and never wrote my thoughts, even though this place brings me peace and comfort and a way to give my troubles to God! This year has brought much heartache, anguish and hurt to family, sons and wife, that I have lost my path. I pray for healing for the anguish and hostility and I pray that my path be shown to me out of the darkness. Pathways healed my soul. It's a gift from God! It's a gift to be here! Thank you for all that I have and all healing. The sunlight shining on me unburdens my soul and gives me new hope."—no name

"Time to stop drinking for good. Starting AA tomorrow. This lovely sanctuary helped to firm my conviction."—no name

"We came here today not knowing what we would see. The beauty we see and the energy here is beyond belief. How I wish my son could see this. I hope and pray that it will still be here in 10 years when he gets set free. He has a great heart, but drugs took him down. Oh God, as I sit here please send him this love I feel here."—no name

Another unique feature of Pathways arrived through the kind of spiritual connection I have come to welcome through my journey.

In late 2007, the Cheyenne River Sioux Tribe needed to disperse the herd of wild mustangs on the tribe's reservation in northern South Dakota. These horses had run wild on 22,000 acres and had not been in contact with humans. A young Lakota man from the reservation had experienced a vision in which Chief Sitting Bull instructed him to save seven stallions from the herd. The horses were to be kept together as symbols of unity and healing for the seven Lakota nations and, more generally, for the unity of all peoples. The young man did not have the land or the financial means to honor Sitting Bull's request. A close friend of mine learned about his vision in October. She felt compelled to find a home for the seven horses and asked me if I would be willing to keep them at the ranch. Chief Sitting Bull, who was killed in 1890, had been in my consciousness since I acquired the ranch in 1993. I had often wondered if he was the one talking to me about the vision for the sanctuary. Was this a coincidence?

I agreed to take the horses, and two days later the seven stallions arrived at the ranch. Chief Sitting Bull's request was honored, and the young man's vision was fulfilled. These seven sacred horses have a very powerful energy. Pathway's visitors enjoy watching the horses graze in the pasture near the path.

They were grazing in a pasture in view of those attending the 2010 dedication ceremony. When the dedication began, they started running in a large circle. The running continued throughout the 40-minute ceremony. At the exact time the dedication ended they stopped running. I had never seen them run like this. Was Sitting Bull present? I don't know for sure, but I think so.

Build it and they will come. Indeed, they have come! One journal entry sums up the Pathways experience.

> "Sky blue Dakota vistas...running mustangs...fields of wild-flowers...shimmering aspen...magnificent and meaningful sculptures."—Ginny D.

Within a year after opening Pathways, I recognized I would not be able to perpetuate the use of this land forever. I own all the assets of Pathways as well as the ranch. I would soon be in my 70s, and I recognized I would not live forever. Physically, that is!

In 2011, I created a South Dakota non-profit corporation—Pathways Spiritual Sanctuary—and I established a seven-person board of directors. The corporation then received the IRS designation of non-profit 501(c)(3) public charity. In 2015, the board created a plan for the perpetuation of the sanctuary. The plan included having the property appraised and it granted the Pathways corporation an option to purchase the entire ranch from me. There was also an employment contract that allowed me to remain as caretaker if the board so desired. Now that the agreements are executed and the appraisal completed, it is our belief that someone, or some entity, will provide the funds to purchase the property and preserve the sanctuary. Our dream is that Pathways continues and will provide its benefits to an increasing number of people. This is our focused intention, so when the time is right our dream will manifest into reality.

And the gate will remain open forever.

Pathways Spiritual Sanctuary

Entry and exit gate at Pathways Spiritual Sanctuary

Entry Prayer of Affirmation with recessed handprints

The Invocation—14-foot tall monumental bronze statue by Buck McCain

Pathway meandering through the aspen grove

Angel and child bronze statue, a tribute to Dave's mother   Artist Lee Luenning

The labryinth modeled after Chartres Cathredral labyrinth built in the 1100s

Windchimes on Harmony Hill at Pathways Spiritual Sanctuary

Exit Prayer of Affirmation with recessed handprints

Seven Sacred Horses at Pathways Spiritual Sanctuary

Mustang horses watching visitors at Pathways Spiritual Sanctuary

Seven rescued mustangs fulfilling vision from Chief Sitting Bull

Seven mustangs in field of wild daisies

Three of the mustang horses enjoying fall grazing

Mustang horses in front of restored original Juso log ranch house built in 1893

The Caretaker at Work at Pathways

Dave planting Timothy grass with no-till-drill

Dave standing by round bales of Timothy hay after successful reseeding

Caretaker Dave ready for repairing fences, a never-ending job

Dave building buck and rail fence at Pathways Spiritual Sanctuary

CHAPTER 29

A Journey to Love
2017

Now in my 70s, I look back on my life and can see how the dots connected. Dad developed Parkinson's disease, which made his right hand tremble. He once told me, "If it wasn't for this, my life would have been different." His tone was one of acceptance and reflection, not regret. I have often thought about his words. What if my mother had not died? What if I had not spent my childhood summer nights in the Turkey Shack? What if I had not moved to South Dakota? Every "what if" in my life would have created a different journey. And if my life at any point had taken a different turn, Pathways Spiritual Sanctuary would not exist. All the dots had to connect.

My dots mark a long journey to love, and included trauma, confusion, questioning and discovery. Now I have returned home—not to the farm in Nebraska but home to the spiritual reality I merged with in the forest. That's where I discovered there is no need to return home. I am home.

I am grateful for the love I received along the way, even though I often didn't recognize or understand it. I am grateful for my experiential discovery of our spiritual world—a world of love, compassion, tolerance and forgiveness. And I am grateful for the healing I have received.

Throughout my spiritual journey I have been skeptical, doubting and questioning. My nature is to seek explanations, but even though I don't understand the "how" of this reality, the spiritual world has become as real to me as the physical world. It has not replaced my physical life—it has enhanced it and helped me understand that all life is connected.

"Mitakuye Oyasin" a Lakota phrase meaning "all my relations" or "we are all related" refers to the interconnectedness of all life. It defines the spiritual world to which I awakened—a world of love, a world without labels, a world beyond differences and beliefs, a world where all life is equal, valued, respected and honored. It's a benevolent world of compassion and forgiveness. And this connection is not just to human life. As I learned in my walk in the forest, when I arrested my foot in mid-air to keep from stepping on a new pine tree, our connection is to all life. I am one with all living things, including our Mother Earth.

In a small clearing in the old forest, a short walk from the main path at Pathways, there is a wood sculpture carved by Stan Engs, a wood carver from the Black Hills. The statue was carved in the 1960s and it's called The Old Philosopher. It is reminiscent of Augusta Rodin's *The Thinker*. I tried to find an appropriate quotation for a plaque for the sculpture but was unsuccessful. One night I asked for help, and I awoke with the instruction to type the following words:

Life, a mere moment,
Floats to the forest floor,
And joins earth's memories.

Live well each moment.
The earth remembers.

As I live the remaining years of my life on this earth, I will honor and respect our connection to our Mother Earth. I will tread more lightly. I will attempt to live more sustainably. The earth does remember.

My journey has led me to believe that while lack of love separates, it is love that connects. It is only through this connection that I can experience compassion, tolerance and forgiveness for myself and all others. Love, compassion, tolerance and forgiveness—the four words given to me on the shoulder of Interstate 70 in the spring of 2009—embody all that I experienced on the spiritual portion of my journey to love. I recognize these words are also the foundation of the major religions of the world. I have a Christian background. The four words summarize the teachings of Jesus that I learned as a boy in church and Sunday school. To me, they are what His life on earth was all about.

I am aware the choices I make every day can come from a place of love. When they do not, I recall the gentle and loving words from *A Course in Miracles*, "My brother, choose once again." I can choose to be loving. I can choose to live with respect and honor. I can choose to recognize that everyone is traveling their own path with the influence of their own histories guiding them. From this understanding I can choose to be more tolerant. I can choose to attempt to view their lives through their eyes. I can then choose to view them with compassion. I can choose to forgive and, in the process, learn that forgiveness is for the forgiver as well as the forgiven.

My journey has also taught me that the choices I make have an impact, visible or invisible, on the world around me. My footsteps reverberate into the future lives of my children, their children and the generations to come. They ripple outward to an expanding circle of influence. I frequently remind myself, "Choose love Dave, choose love."

When I reflect on my journey and the experiences visitors have at Pathways, I have come to believe that striving to live the four words—love, compassion, tolerance and forgiveness—can be the end game for all of us, regardless of which religious or non-religious path we are taking. Could our spiritual reality be as simple as that? I have often wondered, in our effort to comprehend the non-physical spiritual world, if we have made God in our image to facilitate our understanding of the unseen spiritual world. If so, have we inadvertently created complex religions that often separate us rather than connect us?

With the help of my sisters and the insistence of my brother, Dad made the 550-mile trip from Lincoln, Nebraska, to attend the dedication and opening of Pathways Spiritual Sanctuary on July 17, 2010. It meant more to me to have him there at 92 than to have had him attend my football games in high school.

After the ceremony Jim Miller, my Lakota friend and teacher, led guests to form a line to give their thanks. It is a Lakota tradition—similar to a receiving line following a wedding ceremony. During the long procession, Dad stood by my side, shook everyone's hand and received their hugs. After the dedication, Dad and I relaxed on the deck at my house. I thanked him for coming and told him how grateful I was to have him there. I apologized for the long time he had to stand and shake hands. He said the standing didn't bother him. Holding up his right hand, shaking from the Parkinson's, he laughed as he said, "It wasn't too hard shaking their hands either." We both laughed and then looked at each other in silence. Mist formed in our eyes. As was our habit throughout most of our lives, we said nothing. This time we didn't need to. We knew we were getting close to healing our wounds and repairing our relationship. I felt love and compassion for him, and I could see his love for me in his misty eyes. I looked across the meadow to hide my tears. I felt his love.

In late July 2015, I was once again in the tractor seat. This time I was mowing grass in the meadow at Pathways. In a couple of days, this grass would become bales of hay for winter feed. I looked at the hillside on the eastern slope of the meadow where I was sitting under a full moon in 1994—the night the Grandmothers told me I was chosen to protect this land. I looked down at my steel-toed boots and the greasy Carhartt shorts, with pliers protruding from a pocket. I looked up at the frayed brim of the faded John Deere cap that protected my balding head and my old but tanned face. I smiled, and, tipping my cap toward the hillside, I thanked the Grandmothers for choosing me.

As I continued mowing, I reflected on the previous five years. My focus had been on the work necessary to create, open and maintain Pathways. Even though the reward was well worth it, I had been asking for more balance in my life. I longed for a wife to share love, joy and fun. Since my divorce I had dated many women—some were long relationships and one resulted in a second marriage—but the fit was never quite right. I also wanted a wife who felt as I did about Pathways. I wanted someone who would appreciate the words of wisdom on the plaques along the path.

Later that morning, after I finished mowing the meadow west of the mountain stream, I crossed the sanctuary's path. Two women were walking there, so I stopped and got off the tractor to say hello. One of them told me that she was moved by the words on the plaques, and she asked who chose them. As I answered her I couldn't help but notice her radiant smile. After they left I continued thinking about her. I remembered she lived in Wisconsin, but I couldn't recall her name. No way to contact her. But, a few days later I received an email from her on Pathway's website. Attached to the email were several pictures she had taken on her visit. Now I had her name and email address!

There is much more to this story, but most importantly, the glass slipper fit. On September 4, 2016, Jan Avenson Nelson and I were married. I am blessed with our love in my life, and I now know how true love feels in a married relationship.

Dave and Jan Snyder

Had Jan and her sister been 100 feet away when I crossed the walking path, we would have waved to each other and never met. Was our meeting in the hayfield a chance encounter? Probably not.

One day on a return trip from town to buy twine for the hay baler, I stopped for a moment outside the entrance gate to the ranch to watch an elderly couple walk slowly along the path across the meadow. Seeing them walk hand in hand filled me with gratitude for the long journey that led me to create this beautiful sanctuary.

I drove over the cattle guard into the ranch reflecting upon the words on the bronze plaque I had just passed. I installed it in 1996 on the limestone gatepost. It was a quote from *Walden Pond* by Henry David Thoreau:

Only that day dawns to which we are awake.

I continued driving into the ranch, parked in front of the shop, turned off the diesel engine of my Ram pickup, rested my forearms on the steering wheel and read the words on the sign by the door to my shop. It was made of tin and painted John Deere green. The words were John Deere yellow. I smiled as I read:

Still plays with tractors.

Entry gate post

Machine shop on ranch

Epilogue

When I visited Dad and Percy at their farm in Nebraska—while I was having experiences I could not understand or explain—I often talked to them about what was happening to me. They knew I was being honest, and they trusted me. Percy was more receptive than Dad as he was rooted in his Protestant beliefs in good and evil and heaven and hell. He had some difficulty with my experiences, which were about love. But he was always attentive and interested, and he seemed to believe me.

Late one afternoon, after sitting in the living room talking about these events in my life, Percy went to the kitchen to prepare supper. I asked Dad, "Do you really believe I'm actually experiencing these things?" My question was two-fold: first, did he believe me from his Christian viewpoint, and second, I could use his assurance that I was okay and not having mental issues. He was quiet for a moment, sitting in his recliner. He looked toward the kitchen to make sure Percy couldn't hear our conversation. "I have never told this to anyone," he said. "I was on a date with your mother. It was late and past the time she was to be home." "How late was it?" I asked. "Well, I suppose it was about two in the morning." "What!" I exclaimed, echoing the exact words he said to me so many years before, when he had stayed up waiting for my late return from a date. Grinning, I asked him, "What could you possibly be doing that late at night?" Looking like he had been caught, he smiled back and said, "Nothing." We both clearly remembered my one-word reply.

Then my dad told me this story about that date with my mom:

Since it was so late, I decided to take a shortcut on a dirt road that had no gravel. It had rained that evening, but I thought I could get through. I was wrong. I got stuck about two-thirds of the way to the other end. Your mother and I got out of the car and tried everything to get the car unstuck. I had your mother drive while I pushed. We put branches under the wheels so we could get better traction. But nothing worked and I was getting desperate. Your Granddad was a gentle man, but, as you know, he was a big strong man. And back then, he was bigger and stronger than when you knew him.

Finally, I gave up and stood there trying to think of another way out. There had to be a solution. It would be a long walk home. Then I saw the glow of headlights from beyond the hill we had just come over. I could hear the vehicle coming toward us. A pickup came over the hill and stopped beside us. A man got out and said that it looked like we needed some help. He drove his pickup around to the front of my car, backed up, and hooked a chain to the car. He then pulled us to the next intersection where the road had gravel.

Dave, by the time I got out of the car, he had already backed up and unhooked the chain. I thanked him and took out my wallet. He held up his hand saying he did not want any money. He told me that someday I would be in the position to help someone else and, assuming I would offer help, that was all the payment he wanted. He got in his pickup and drove off.

We got back in the car and sped off to your Granddad's house. We couldn't believe our luck. What were the odds that someone with a truck and chain would come along in the middle of the night just when we needed him?

When I returned home and got into bed I thought again about the odds of that happening. The man was quite old, and a stranger. I didn't know many people in that neighborhood and I wished I had looked at his license plate.

The next morning, the old man was still on my mind. After I ate breakfast and finished my chores I drove back to the road where we had been stuck. I saw our tracks and, since the road had dried some and I was driving a pickup, I decided to drive to where we were stuck. Our tracks were there as well as our footprints. I could see the evidence of our futile efforts to get unstuck—including the branches. But Dave, as I looked around I couldn't believe it. There were no other tire tracks except my car's tracks. Nowhere. Not up either hill. I drove back to the end of the road where we had unhooked—no tracks.

I drove to your Granddad's house and got your mother. I told her what I had seen. She got in the pickup and we went back to the mud road. I had hoped the other tracks would somehow be there, but they weren't. Only our car tracks and those of my pickup. We sat there in my pickup for a while in silence. I remember your mother got out and walked around in front of my pickup. She walked slowly, deep in thought, shaking her head in disbelief.

I got out and joined her. We just stood there in silence. I remember she finally looked at me and asked, "How could this be?" I had no answer. I couldn't even answer her today if she was here. I assume she probably knows the answer now, but I still don't.

I sat in stunned silence. Dad leaned forward in his chair, got up and headed for the kitchen. As he passed me he said, "So, yes Dave, I believe you."

Dave with his dad at the Turkey Shack 2009
55 years since Dave's first night in the tin shed

Acknowledgments

First and foremost I express my gratitude for the guidance I received that resulted in the creation of Pathways Spiritual Sanctuary. That same guidance asked me to write this book. Despite my fervent reservations about my capabilities to write a book, I was assured that I would receive the help I needed. And I did.

I thank Bill Harlan for his tremendous help copyediting and Mandy Knight for proofreading.

A special thank you to Bonnie Malterer who volunteered many hours helping me with the wording and proper grammar.

Thank you to Jan Camp for urging me to write the book by telling it through my stories.

A special expression of gratitude to long-time friend Trudy Severson who spent countless hours listening, taking notes and encouraging me during the six years it took to create this work. Without Trudy this book would not exist.

To cousin Teresa Rennick, my thanks for your help, support and edits.

To Amanda Shaykett for expanding my view of the spiritual world and alerting me to the need to rescue the seven mustangs.

I am grateful to all who have been a part of my journey to love. This includes my daughters Carly and Jaime who stayed by my side during the turbulent years and have supported me on my spiritual journey and writing this book, my good friend Joan Irwin who counseled and supported me during some very difficult years, and my business partner of 23 years Dave Luers and the employees of D & D Farms.

Thank you to my fellow Pathways Spiritual Sanctuary Board of Directors and Officers: Carly Ericson, Jaime Hamm, Jeff Parker, David Schwietert, Trudy Severson, Jan Snyder and Steve Zellmer.

I give my thanks to the many others who moved into and out of my life during my long journey and to the visitors to Pathways Spiritual Sanctuary.

A special thanks to my wife Jan Avenson Snyder for her unwavering belief that this book needed to be published. Without her support, encouragement and help this book would not have come to fruition.

We are all connected.

The Turkey Shack book may be purchased at:

On site: **Pathways Spiritual Sanctuary**

On line: www.pathwaysspiritualsanctuary.org

Net proceeds from the sale of *The Turkey Shack* shall be used for the care, maintenance and further development of Pathways Spiritual Sanctuary.

ABOUT THE AUTHOR

Dave Snyder grew up on a family farm in southeast Nebraska and had a career in production agriculture. He moved to South Dakota in 1980 where he and his partner continued their farming operations in the states of South Dakota, Nebraska, Montana and Colorado. In 2000 Dave retired to a small ranch in the Black Hills of South Dakota. In 2010 he built Pathways Spiritual Sanctuary on a portion of that ranch where he and his wife Jan reside.

CPSIA information can be obtained
at www.ICGtesting.com
Printed in the USA
LVHW011951021021
699320LV00006B/18